Girls for God:

soul perspectives

Girls for God:
soul perspectives

KATIE WOOD

Text copyright © Katie Wood 2009
The author asserts the moral right
to be identified as the author of this work

Published by
The Bible Reading Fellowship
15 The Chambers, Vineyard
Abingdon OX14 3FE
United Kingdom
Tel: +44 (0)1865 319700
Email: enquiries@brf.org.uk
Website: www.brf.org.uk

ISBN 978 0 85746 070 7
First published 2009
This edition 2012
10 9 8 7 6 5 4 3 2 1 0

Acknowledgments
Unless otherwise stated, scripture quotations are taken from the Contemporary English
Version of the Bible published by HarperCollins Publishers, copyright © 1991, 1992, 1995
American Bible Society.

The paper used in the production of this publication was supplied by mills that source their
raw materials from sustainably managed forests. Soy-based inks were used in its printing and
the laminate film is biodegradable.

A catalogue record for this book is available from the British Library

Printed in Singapore by Craft Print International Ltd

Contents

Introduction

Being a teenager is not an easy thing at the best of times. There are so many changes, like moving schools, getting jobs or even starting university, and there are a lot of stresses, too, like exams, arguments and trying to get a boyfriend. Some of this is pretty scary but a lot of it is really exciting, too.

In this book I aim to provide tips and advice for different situations, drawn from my experiences and those of my friends— but the real advice doesn't come from me, it comes from God, as found in the Bible. You may already have a relationship with God, which is great, but equally you might not have really thought about it. Either way, the Bible is a fantastic book of advice. It's not all 'thou shalt not…' and in many ways it's really practical and can help us in all kinds of circumstances, many centuries after it was written. I have included lots of Bible verses (all from the Contemporary English Version), which have helped me through different stuff I've found myself facing. These verses are arranged into sections for specific times and events in life.

Of course, the other way that we can access the real advice that comes from God is through prayer. I have included some prayers that I have written for various times when you might need help but don't know how to ask for it, when prayer seems difficult or when you just don't know how to start. Obviously, you may find that your own prayers are more relevant for you.

Unlike many books of this nature, I am not going to mention my university degree or any other 'official' qualifications that give me the authority to discuss the matters involved here. The main reason for this is that I don't have any. What I do have, however, is experience and the fact that I myself am a teenager. At the time of writing, I am an average 18-year-old studying in the sixth form, worrying about universities and stressing about my friends. I am a Christian, although I only became one when I was 16. I don't know how I survived before I had a relationship with God, because now

I know that he is in charge and has a plan for my life—whatever that turns out to be.

This book came about by chance (or perhaps not—call it what you will), as it started with a little notebook in which I wrote down Bible verses that I found helpful. Then I wrote a prayer for an assembly for my sixth form, which my (non-Christian) friend read. She told me it was exactly what needed to be said. I realised that, although it seemed simple to me, prayer is something that many people find difficult to pinpoint or talk about—and so I hope that this book might get you thinking.

At the beginning of each chapter I have included a verse from the Bible and a simple prayer. I then discuss a slightly longer Bible extract, along with my thoughts and comments. Then follows another prayer and an encouraging Bible verse to remember, along with some points for reflection. You can read through a chapter when you feel it particularly applies to you, and I hope that you will return again and again to the Bible verses and prayers as starting points for your own reflection. Try to learn some of the short verses by heart, as I find it so helpful when they pop into your head later, when you need them most. You could use the longer Bible extracts and questions for reflection for discussions in a youth group or among your friends.

I hope that this book may give you some help, inspiration and encouragement and I sincerely hope that all the glory will go to God.

When you need encouragement

What the Bible says

Christ encourages you, and his love comforts you.
God's Spirit unites you.

PHILIPPIANS 2:1

Dear Lord, please be with me when I am feeling discouraged. I thank you, Lord, that you are here for me and that you do give us encouragement when we need it, and that all we have to do is ask for it. Lord, please fill me with your love and encourage me to continue living my life for you and in the way that you want. Amen

I find Philippians a very encouraging bit of the Bible—which is not surprising, as it is a letter that Paul wrote to Christians at Philippi, a city in ancient Greece, specifically to encourage them. In Philippians 3:12–16, Paul, one of the most inspiring and dedicated of the early Christians, admits that he isn't perfect and that he hasn't yet arrived at where he wants to be. However, he says he knows that Jesus is with him and so he forgets everything in the past and simply focuses on where he's heading—heaven, the prize that God gives us simply for believing and trusting in him. He encourages all of us to keep focused on this prize in the same way, so that we can make the most of the encouragement that God provides.

How reassuring is that? To think that even Paul recognises the fact that he, like us, is not perfect! At this stage in his life, Paul has been put in prison for his faith, yet he can still think positively, knowing that God will help him to slog on with what needs to be done. It's this focus on his reward in heaven that allows him to have such an amazing attitude.

You may be stressing out and feeling discouraged because the goals you have in your mind are about meeting homework deadlines or slaving away at your job, but, if we have this ultimate goal of heaven in mind, it will probably feel a lot easier to keep going.

When you're feeling fed up, who better to give you encouragement than the Creator of the universe? So when you need a pick-me-up, turn to him. Your problems might seem insignificant compared with the job of making the whole world, but God really does care— it says so all through the Bible.

Throughout the Gospels, Jesus keeps referring to himself as a shepherd, such as in John 10:11, where he says, 'I am the good shepherd, and the good shepherd gives up his life for his sheep.' This shows to what extent he will look after his flock—meaning us. It doesn't mean that we have to wear woolly fleeces. It means that Jesus is looking out for us and that, even if just one of us gets lost, he will rescue us and help us to keep on track. Just look at the story of Paul (who was called Saul at first): he used to go around killing Christians, but Jesus spoke to him on the road to Damascus and showed him what to do, so he gave his life to Christ, changed his name and began spreading the gospel.

Unlike most people, God will always want to be around you and spend time with you, so, when you feel that you're being a drain on the rest of the company, tune in to God's presence, because he's there to listen to you or just to be quiet with you—whatever you want. Everyone goes through times when they really don't feel like doing anything, even getting out of bed, which means that when you're finding life too much of a struggle, you are so not alone!

When you're feeling discouraged about anything, another really helpful thing to do is to share it with someone. If you're a Christian, try someone (or several people) in your church; if you don't feel you can claim to be a Christian, just talk to a friend or family member— anybody who you know will support you. Try not to worry about approaching them, as they're bound to be flattered that you went to them rather than somebody else. You can pray that God will lead you to the right person and that he will give you the right words to say.

Ask this person to encourage you (and, if possible, pray for you) in connection with the specific issues that you need help with. In my experience, the more people praying about something, the better it goes. It will really give you a boost, too, to know that somebody else cares enough to do this and that they're thinking of you. If nothing else, if another person knows that you're discouraged, they can at least try to cheer you up...

Lord, at times the marathon of life seems so difficult to run, and we get worn out so quickly and sidetracked by the ways of the world. Lord, please help us to realise that, with you at our side, we can never reach a dead end, and you will help to redirect us whenever we stray from the course. We thank you, Lord, that you always offer us the strength, love and support that we need. Please help us to keep running the race for you. Amen

※ To remember

> You know that many runners enter a race, and only one of them wins the prize. So run to win!

> I CORINTHIANS 9:24

※ Reflection

- What do you think heaven is like? Focus on this, your ultimate goal.
- What do you think makes God proud of you?
- How can you make him feel like this more often?

When you're worried

What the Bible says

God cares for you, so turn all your worries over to him.

I PETER 5:7

Dear God, please help me when I'm feeling worried. Help me to know that I can come to you with any problems I have, no matter what they are or how silly I think I am for worrying about them. Thank you, God, for loving us all and for being there for us at these difficult times. Amen

Worry affects all of us, including those people in the Bible who lived over 2000 years ago. In Matthew 6:25–34, Jesus speaks about worry. He says that we shouldn't worry about our lives, as God looks after everything. He tells us not to worry about what we have to eat, drink or wear, as life is more important. He tells us to look at the birds, which don't worry about any of these things, yet still have enough to eat and drink because God takes care of them.

He then tells us to think about flowers: they don't worry about what they wear, yet they can be amazingly beautiful. God created each of us, just like he created the flowers and birds, and he loves us even more than them. So, if he does those great things for them, he'll do even greater things for us. If we put God's work first, everything else will just come naturally. Jesus tells us not to worry about tomorrow but just to concentrate on each day as it comes.

When you're feeling worried, it can burn a hole through your personality. It eats you up inside and stops you enjoying life. What's important to remember, though, is that we mustn't worry about being worried! It sounds crazy but, when you're worrying, try telling yourself that it's natural to worry about stuff and that everyone feels like that from time to time.

I'm sure that the best thing to remember when you're worried is that God loves you. That might or might not seem obvious but, when you're really panicking it's actually easy to forget the obvious stuff, even if you hear it all the time, at church or youth group or wherever. If you keep reassuring yourself that this is true—God really does love you—then you should start to feel calmer.

It's also important to remember that, because God loves you, he wants to help you. So when you are really fretting, pray to him, take your problem to him and he will help you through it. He may not take the problem away immediately but he'll certainly reassure you so that you feel you can cope with it better.

Jesus tells us not to worry about the details of life because we simply cannot control them. I find that especially helpful, as it can be tempting to worry about tiny little things that seem enormous to us but that we cannot do anything about. When we realise that although we can't be in total control of life, God can, the problems can suddenly seem less overwhelming. We can consciously hand our worries over and let him help us through.

Look at Moses in the desert. He was sure that he and his people would not have enough food, yet every night God sent them enough manna (sweet, wafer-like bread) to get them through the next day. They had to trust in him to give them the food each night, because if they stored more than they needed for one day, it turned bad. We read in Exodus 16:20 that 'some of them disobeyed, but the next morning what they kept was stinking and full of worms'. This is like us not listening to God but choosing to worry instead; if we just trust in God, he will provide us with all that we need.

Sometimes, when you're worrying, you can't seem to concentrate on anything else. Even when you try praying to God, you don't feel that he's listening. This is probably because your worries are crowding your head and stopping his voice from reaching you. When this happens, simply focus on listening. Find a place where you can be in silence and try to relax, doing whatever you find helpful—playing music, breathing deeply, even having a bath. Then ask God to speak to you and give you guidance, and listen to hear what he brings to your mind.

I once heard someone say that God gives us the ability to cope with everything that happens in one particular day. So when we start to worry about things from the past or in the future, we feel unable to cope because we've already used up all our coping ability on today's problems. As Jesus said, we should try to concentrate on what we have to deal with at the moment and trust that God will look after us and provide for us tomorrow, when it comes. At the risk of sounding like an old lady—smile, it might not happen! If God knows that you really won't be able to cope with a situation, he won't put you through it.

However, sometimes the thing that we're dreading does happen, and it can feel as if God is abandoning us or, at least, is not listening. But try to trust in him; he does have a plan for you and he will make sure that the right things happen for you. If there's a future event that I'm dreading, I sometimes pray that God won't put me through it—and it happens anyway. Then I find that it's nowhere near as bad as I thought it would be, and I actually gain something from the experience. God will always give us the strength we need to get through any situation. Isaiah 40:31 says, 'Those who trust the Lord will find new strength. They will be strong like eagles soaring upward on wings.'

Father, please ease the horrible feeling of worry that can eat us up inside. Thank you that we can talk to you whenever we are worried, but please help us to be able to listen to you, too. Thank you that you always provide us with what we need to face whatever worries us. I pray that you will help me to remember this, and to focus on you when I start to worry. Amen

❋ To remember

When I was really suffering, I prayed to the Lord. He answered my prayer, and took my worries away.

PSALM 118:5

※ Reflection

- What are the actual issues that are worrying you? Break them down into manageable chunks and write them down.
- If someone came to you with these worries, what would you advise them?
- How do you think other people have dealt with the things that are worrying you at the moment?

When something good has happened

What the Bible says

I praise the Lord for answering my prayers and saving me.

PSALM 118:21

Heavenly Father, thank you so much for [what has happened]. I feel so happy that you have blessed me with this. I pray that you will help me to remember how good I feel right now so that I can draw on it when I'm feeling down. Please help me not to forget to thank you for all that you do for me, and show me how I can share my joy with others. Amen

The psalms are full of people praising God for all the fantastic things he's done. Psalm 103 in particular looks at 'the Lord's wonderful love'. Here, David (the teenager who killed the giant Goliath with a tiny stone and later became the king of Israel) talks about everything that God has done for him. He talks about how the Lord forgives our sins, heals us when we are sick, protects us from death, provides for our needs, gives us strength, gives justice to those who are mistreated (I feel like I need to pause for breath!) and teaches us right and wrong.

Next, he goes on about God's amazing characteristics, such as the fact that he is merciful, kind, patient, never stops loving us, doesn't get angry, doesn't remind us of what we do wrong and doesn't punish us, even though we deserve it. Then he says that God loves us more than the distance between heaven and earth, that he's taken our sins from us further than the distance between east and west and that he is as kind to us as parents are to their children.

And it doesn't stop there. David tells us that the Lord is always kind to the people who worship him, that he keeps his promises even to their children (and theirs, and theirs!), that God created heaven, which he rules, and even the angels obey him. Finally David tries to rally together every single one of God's creatures to get them to worship him together, which makes the exclamation marks go a bit crazy on the page!

It's fantastic when something great has happened that makes you feel like shouting out at the top of your voice, like David sounds as if he's doing here. But think about it: something this great has happened—to all of us. If you read through Psalm 103, you can see that David doesn't say 'he provides for *my* needs' but 'he provides for *our* needs' (v. 5). All the way through, he talks about everything that God has done for 'us', which includes you and me.

Even if you're not sure exactly what you believe about God, doesn't it seem pretty amazing that someone loves us enough to do for us what that psalm tells us God does? And there's even more. God came to earth himself in the form of his Son, Jesus, to die so that we have the hope of eternal life. So whatever the good thing is that's happened to you, try to remember that there is always something even better, as John 3:16 tells us: 'God loved the people of this world so much that he gave his only Son, so that everyone who has faith in him will have eternal life and never really die.'

When we're happy and feel like celebrating, it is good to remember who is in overall control of absolutely everything. It is really easy to read the Bible only when we need advice, or pray only when we want something. But how would you feel if you really loved someone and would do anything for them, yet they only spoke to you to ask a favour? How often do we treat God this way?

It can be hard to remember God at times when all you want to do is shout your head off or dance with joy or ring up your friends for a long chat about your good news. Try not to forget about God—he loves you so much because he made you, and he wants to share your happiness with you.

When you're celebrating about something, try to take a few moments out to sit in peace and quiet by yourself. Think about what has happened and allow that happiness to fill you up. Try reading some psalms (such as Psalm 63 and 111) or put on a Christian worship CD and listen to the words or read once again through the list above of all that David was thankful for. Focus on these amazing things as well as your own good news, so that they can add to your happiness.

Then pray to God, thanking him for everything he's done for you, including whatever it is that has made you so happy. By doing this, you're allowing God to join in your happiness with you.

Lord God, thank you so much for everything you've done for me and thank you even more that you sent Jesus to die for me. Lord, please help me to remember to spend time with you even when I'm busy celebrating something great that has happened. Help me to remember that you are the one who created everything and that all good things come from you. Thank you again, Lord. Amen

❋ To remember

I never stop thanking my God for being kind enough to give… Christ Jesus.

1 CORINTHIANS 1:4

❋ Reflection

- What is the best thing that has ever happened to you? How did it make you feel? Write down these feelings somewhere private and keep them to look back on when you're not feeling so happy.
- How do you feel when someone you care about shares some good news with you? How can you remind yourself to share your own good news with God?

When you've messed up

What the Bible says

'I will treat [my followers] with kindness, even though they are wicked. I will forget their sins.'

HEBREWS 8:12

Dear God, I've messed up badly and I feel so awful about it. I truly am sorry for [what I did], Lord; please forgive me. I thank you that you not only forgive our sins but that you forget about them, too. Lord, please help me to move on from this and help me not to do the same thing again. Please let me feel you with me; encourage me and help me to remember that whenever I do mess up, you still love me and you will keep on forgiving me. Amen

Whenever I feel bad because I've done something wrong, I find the story of Peter so encouraging. Peter was one of Jesus' disciples who followed him and really loved him. When Jesus tells Peter, at the last supper, that he will deny even knowing him, Peter is shocked and cannot believe that he will do such a thing to his master and friend (see Mark 14:29, where Peter says, 'Even if all the others reject you, I never will!') Yet, when it comes to the crucifixion, Peter does deny that he knows Jesus, not just once but three times.

Later, once Jesus has risen from the dead, he appears to the disciples while they are fishing. Peter is the first to recognise him as their Lord and runs to greet him by jumping in the water (John 21:7). Jesus invites Peter to come and eat with him and then gives him instructions to look after Jesus' followers.

In this story, we've got someone who lets Jesus down repeatedly, but, when Jesus comes back from the dead, he doesn't shout at Peter and punish him. Instead, he just asks him to come and eat with him, showing his forgiveness. He will do exactly the same for each and every one of us.

When you've messed up and are feeling awful, as if you've really let God down, just remember that he still loves you despite everything you do wrong. You might feel that you don't want to talk to God any more because you're so ashamed, but don't follow that route. God already knows anyway, and he is unshockable. So talk to him and tell him how sorry you are. Besides, you will not be the first person who has messed up badly.

Remember that God forgives us for everything we do, if we ask for his forgiveness. Why else would he have sent Jesus? There would be no point in sending his Son to die for our sin if we didn't sin. Of course, that doesn't mean we're free to do whatever we like, as sin gets in the way of our relationship with God, but the point is that we're not perfect and we will fail, but God's ready to forgive us when we pray to him.

Once we've asked for God's forgiveness, we can believe that he has forgiven us, even if we end up making the same mistake again. 1 John 1:9 says, 'If we confess our sins to God, he can always be trusted to forgive us and take our sins away.'

Throughout the Bible there are examples of people who messed up, but still God forgave them. One example is Jonah. God told Jonah to go to a city called Nineveh (I don't know how it's pronounced either!) to give the people there a message, but Jonah ran in the opposite direction because he thought the job would be too hard. He got on a ship to sail far away, but God made sure that he ended up being thrown overboard, where he was gobbled up by a big fish. God caused this fish to throw up Jonah on to the shore, where God again told him to go to Nineveh to deliver his message. Jonah said how sorry he was, went and told everyone the message, and it was a lot easier than he thought. So this shows us that, even when we disobey God, he can still use us in an amazing way if we turn back to him.

You might find it helpful to write a letter to God, explaining what you did wrong and asking him to forgive you. Once you've done this, rip up the piece of paper, slowly and taking deep breaths. Then throw the paper away and forget about it, as a sign that God has forgiven you and that he will forget you ever did it. Ask God to fill you with his peace.

Once you have asked for God's forgiveness, if you find that you still feel bad about what happened, try to talk to somebody about it. Speak to somebody you trust, such as a family member, a close friend, a youth leader or somebody else from church, maybe even a teacher. Try not to feel embarrassed by what you've done, as you'd be surprised how many people have done it before you.

If you've done something bad to somebody else, speak to them and ask their forgiveness. This is a really hard thing to do but, if you ask God to help you through it, he will give you the words to say and the courage to say them. Even if the other person finds it difficult to forgive you straight away, remember that God has forgiven you, and you can pray for your relationship with the other person to be healed over time.

Heavenly Father, I thank you that you love me, no matter what. I thank you that you will forgive me no matter what I do. Please be with me, Lord, and help me to sort everything out that's happened because of what I did wrong, especially my relationships with any others involved. And please help me to be strong. In Jesus' name. Amen

☼ To remember

> God did not keep back his own Son, but he gave him for us. If God did this, won't he freely give us everything else?

ROMANS 8:32

☼ Reflection

- How do you feel when someone you really care about does something wrong?

- What do you think is the best way to apologise to God?
- Think about the way you've messed up. How can you make sure you don't do the same thing again?

When you want someone to feel special

What the Bible says

A friendly smile makes you happy.

PROVERBS 15:30

Dear God, thank you so much for those people in our lives who are really special to us, those people who make each day seem brighter, who make each memory that much more unforgettable, who make each moment more joyful. Please help us to remember that if it wasn't for you we'd never have any of these people, as you created them all. Amen

The book of Ecclesiastes is all about a man thinking hard about life. In chapter 4 and verses 9–12, he thinks about what it's like to have friends. He says that it's better to have a friend than to be alone because friendship helps you to enjoy what you have. If you fall, a friend will help you back up again, but if you don't have a friend, then you're in trouble.

He goes on to say that, if friends stick together, they can literally keep each other warm and that someone might be able to beat up one of you but not both of you together. He quotes from an old saying that a rope made of three strands is hard to break, so the more friends you have, the stronger you will be.

This is a really encouraging part of the Bible (even though a lot of Ecclesiastes can get a bit depressing, as it talks elsewhere about life being meaningless) because it not only makes us appreciate our friends but also shows us how we can be great friends to others. It shows that we should always stick with our friends, no matter what, as good friends will help us up when we have trouble, make us a stronger person and generally help us to enjoy life more.

In several places in the Gospels, Jesus tells us that we should appreciate our friends and realise that they are more important than things like money. Check out John 12:1–8, where Jesus tells Judas not to worry about wasting money, as the woman's love for him is more important. It's the age-old idea that money can't buy you love, and (besides the fact that it always makes me want to sing the Beatles song) it really is great advice to remember.

Think of two women: one is rich, lives in a huge house, has hundreds of pairs of designer shoes and has a different coloured mobile to suit her every mood, but she spends all day sitting around by herself because she doesn't have any friends. Then think about another woman, who is poor and lives in a small rented flat with threadbare carpets and outdated, secondhand clothes. Yet this woman's house is never empty because she always has friends round and, instead of expensive interior design, they decorate the flat with constant laughter. Which woman do you think is happier?

If you've got great friends, that's fantastic. As Paul says when he talks about love in 1 Corinthians 13, this kind of love will last even when everything else fades away. It reminds us of God's love for us, which is even stronger. No matter what happens to us, whether we have millions of friends or hardly any, Jesus will always be our friend. Whether or not we have tons of designer clothes, God will always care for us.

It's good to let your friends know how much you care about them, as it'll make you all feel good and make your friendship stronger, so that when any of you experience problems, you'll be able to help each other through them all the better. One important lesson I've learned over the last few years is never to take your friends for granted, because if you suddenly didn't have them, you'd miss them a lot.

Make your friends feel special by sending them a text or email with some encouraging words, maybe even a Bible verse. Some good verses to try are Philippians 1:3–4, also 4:14 and 23; 1 Corinthians 1:9; Psalms 45:2 and 37:24; 1 Thessalonians 5:16; Proverbs 15:30; or Colossians 3:14. There are loads more, and it just goes to show

how important friends were to many of the different people in the Bible. Alternatively, you could send your friends a line or two of a song that makes you think of them or reminds you of a fun time you've had together.

You don't have to spend a fortune to make your friends feel special, either. If they've got a special occasion coming up or are going through a hard time, why not make them a card or bake them some fairy cakes (you can find ideas for both of these on the Internet pretty easily) to say well done, wish them luck or simply let them know you're thinking of them. I know that I always find these kinds of gifts the most special, as my friends have spent time on them as well as money.

Pray regularly for your friends, that God will help them through any situations where they're struggling, that he will help them to be happy and bless your friendship with them.

Heavenly Father, thank you so much for the special people you've put in my life. Thank you for all of the times when they've helped me through difficult situations. Please help me to be ready to help them when they go through hard times, too. Lord, help me not to take them for granted and help me to remember to show them how much they mean to me. Amen

❋ To remember

Someone might be able to beat up one of you, but not both of you. As the saying goes, 'A rope made from three strands of cord is hard to break.'

ECCLESIASTES 4:12

❋ Reflection

- What is the nicest thing that a friend has ever done for you?
- What was it about it that made you feel so special?

- What do you think are the qualities that make a really great friend?

When people around you need help

What the Bible says

I pray that the Lord Jesus will be kind to you.

I CORINTHIANS 16:23

Dear Lord, please be with me when those around me need help. Please help me not to feel burdened by their problems, but let me be able to help in whatever way I can. I thank you that you are there to help anyone who asks, and I pray that you will help me to encourage these people to trust in your help. Amen

Throughout his letter to Titus, Paul gives good advice to his friend, who was leading a church in Crete at the time. In chapter 3, verses 1–11, Paul shows him how the people of God should live. He says that they shouldn't be rebellious and should always be ready to help, holding back from saying cruel things or arguing. He says that they (Titus and himself) used to be stupid and disobedient, always giving in to loads of bad desires, and that because of this they hated everyone and everyone hated them back. But then he talks about how God has made them clean and acceptable.

Paul then says that this message is useful to everyone and that we should all use testimonies like these to encourage others. He also warns, though, that we shouldn't get into pointless arguments about things that don't matter. When we come across people who are doing something wrong, we should gently and sensitively warn them about it, but be careful not to get involved so that we aren't brought down too.

What Paul is getting at here is, firstly, that if you stick to doing things the right way yourself, then (a) others will respect you and (b) you'll set a good example, so others can learn from you. Secondly, if you are always ready and willing to put yourself out for others, people around you will be more likely to come to you for advice, and God can use you to reach those who need his love. Lastly, in verse 8, Paul shows us that we can use our own experiences to help people, by reminding them that they are not alone in whatever they're experiencing.

A good way to make sure you're prepared to help others is by reading part of the Bible every day, even if it's only for ten minutes, because that will help you to tune in to how the really great people in the Bible (especially Jesus) helped others. Also, make sure you spend some time praying every day, keeping open your direct line to God, so that when you come to pray for (and even with) other people, it is second nature to you.

When you suspect that somebody needs help with something, pray about it first. Ask God to show you how you can help them; ask him to give you the words to say and the courage to say them. Then try approaching that person. Don't go barging up to them and demand that they talk to you; Paul tells us that we should treat people gently (see Galatians 6:1). If you don't see the person regularly, you could try giving them a phone call or email for a chat or invite them to hang out. Judge your next steps by their response: if they seem eager to talk, let them and listen to them without interrupting until they've finished. Often, just talking will make people feel better. Say a quick prayer to God for help before you give them any advice.

It might be that their problem isn't something you feel able to deal with. If so, try to lead them in the direction of someone who can help—maybe a teacher or other trusted adult, such as a church member. You can continue to help and care for them by praying for them regularly.

Even if you know you can't give much practical help, you could have a look through a Bible (or this book) and see if you can find a verse to share with them. You could scribble it on a piece of paper and give it to them or just leave it somewhere they're likely to find it, praying that God will speak to them and encourage them through it. This is also something that you can do if, after you've approached the person, you find they don't really want to talk.

Remember, if they seem to want to be left alone, give them their own space. They will talk to someone when they feel ready, and knowing that you've offered to listen should remind them that they're not alone. Keep praying for them and, if you feel comfortable, ask others to pray for them too. Don't forget, though, that they may not want people to know they're having problems, so be very careful that you don't go blabbing too much!

Heavenly Father, when I am trying to help others, please help me to know what to say and how I can best support them. Help me to remember to keep praying for them, even if they don't want to talk, and help me to deal with matters as sensitively as I can. Please give me the wisdom to know when to speak and when to listen. Lord, please speak through me to other people, so that they can be reached by your wonderful love when they most need it. Amen

※ To remember

I pray that God will take care of all your needs with the wonderful blessings that come from Christ Jesus!

PHILIPPIANS 4:19

※ Reflection

- What is the best advice that somebody has given you?
- Think about the person whom you're most likely to turn to for advice. What makes them so approachable?
- How can you make yourself approachable like that?

When you're going through a difficult time

What the Bible says

If you honour the Lord, his angel will protect you.

PSALM 34:7

Lord, stuff is so difficult right now; I just don't know how to cope with it. Please show me if there is anything I can do to make it better. Please help me to be able to put all my trust in you. Lord, I thank you so much that you are always there for me when times are good as well as when times get tough. Amen

The book of Isaiah is all about the hope that comes after doom for Israel, and Isaiah 35:1–7 talks in poetry about how 'God's splendour' will be revealed when he acts to deliver his people after their exile in Babylon. It says that thirsty deserts will be happy and celebrate as flowers grow there: they will sing with joy so beautifully that everyone will see how wonderful God is. The passage then tells anyone who is weak, sad or worried to cheer up and not be afraid because God is coming, and he will take care of their enemies for them.

People who are blind will be able to see, people who are deaf will be able to hear, people who can't walk will jump around, those who can't talk will start to shout and water will pour through the desert. The places suffering drought will turn to lakes with fountains, and grass will grow in the driest, most horrible places where only wild dogs went before.

Even in the most unlikely of settings, good things can happen because of God. Some parts of our world today may seem completely bleak and desolate but, one day, when God knows it's the right time, he will make everything better again. So even when you feel as if joy is completely impossible, you can hope that God will one day act to transform things. We need to remember, though, that God will act at the right time. When life is tough, you just want it to change as quickly as possible, and it can be easy to despair if you pray and God doesn't take the problem away immediately.

When we are having trouble, it's helpful to realise that we may need difficult times to help us learn, to help us grow as individuals and in our faith. Think about a toddler who can't walk yet. If his parents carried him around all the time, he would never start walking for himself. If his parents leave the room and he cannot reach his favourite toy (which probably seems like a huge problem to someone that young), he will try to get to it by himself. It will be hard, but it will help him to learn to walk. Although they're not in the room, his parents haven't abandoned him, because if he gets into difficulties he will call and they will come.

This is a lot like us: if we never experience problems, we'll never learn how to deal with them. When we first try to cope, like a toddler learning to walk, we may well stumble, but God will help us to get back up again. Like the parents of the child, he hasn't abandoned us—we just need to shout. At the time, it can be difficult to see how anything good can come out of our problems, but once we've come through them it can all start to make sense.

For example, it could be that a friendship or relationship with a boyfriend has come to an end, and that can feel really difficult to go through. Just trust in God and remember that everything happens for a reason. It might be that it's God's will for you to mend the relationship and become a friend or girlfriend to that person again, in which case you can trust that it will happen at the right time, and listen to what God tells you. It might be, though, that the person involved is not someone you should have in your life right now—for any number of reasons. We can't understand what God is thinking, but he knows what we are thinking, and he knows what's best for us, so, hard as it may be, we need to try to trust him and take comfort from the words he gives us in the Bible. When

I recently thought that my boyfriend and I might break up, God led me to this verse: 'Just be patient and don't worry about what will happen. He won't rest until everything is settled today!' (Ruth 3:18)—and the situation was settled that day!

Being a Christian doesn't protect you from having difficulties in life—nothing can. Having a faith can give you some protection, though, in that you have a relationship with God. You have someone you can always depend on, who will always listen to you and can give you advice when you need it. When we're going through a tough time, we should remember to talk through the situation with God in prayer. He may not take the problems away, but he will make them more manageable by listening and then showing us how to start coping.

When we pray in times of trouble, we tend to bombard God with our problems and forget to listen as well. A way round this is to go to a place where you can be alone, in quiet, and start by telling God everything that's bothering you. You can just state the problem once, just as it is, then sit (or stand or lie, whatever is most comfortable) in silence and let God enter that space. Then see if what pops into your head feels like some advice or encouragement from God.

Everyone has difficult times in their lives; just try to be patient, rely on God and stick it out. We can trust that the situation will work out for the best in the end, even if it's not the outcome we want. Sometimes the outcome we want would actually be bad for us, and so God takes care of us, like a good parent, by making the right thing happen.

Father, please be with me in this difficult time and let me focus on your words in the Bible and on my relationship with you to help me through. Lord, please help me to learn from this time so that when I'm on the other side I can understand why I went through it and use what I've learned to help others. Help me never to forget that you want what's best for me and that you love me. Amen

✳ To remember

The Lord has a reason for everything he does.

PROVERBS 16:4

✳ Reflection

- Think about someone who is really successful. What problems do you think they might have faced before they got to where they are today?
- What was the last big problem you had? Can you think now of something good that came from it?
- Can you think of a situation where you or someone you know got something that they'd really wanted and then regretted it?

When you feel tempted

What the Bible says

Even if you think you can stand up to temptation, be careful not to fall.

I CORINTHIANS 10:12

Dear Lord, when I am being tempted, please give me the strength to resist and to do what you want me to do instead. Lord, I'm sorry for the times when I've given in to the temptations I face, but I thank you that you are always ready to forgive me. Please help me to remember to turn to you when I am struggling with temptation. Amen

Don't worry about being tempted: it happens to all of us and it happened to Jesus, too. We read about this in Matthew 4:1–11, when Jesus went without eating for 40 days to show his love for God. When he was really hungry, the devil came to him and said that if he was God's Son, he would be able to turn the stones into bread. Jesus replied that the scriptures (which meant the Old Testament) said that people couldn't only live on bread; they needed the word of God, too.

The devil then took Jesus to the city of Jerusalem and made him stand on the top of the temple. The devil told him that if he was God's Son he could jump off, as the scriptures said that God's angels would catch him. Jesus replied that the scriptures also say that you shouldn't try to test God. After this, the devil took Jesus to the top of a mountain and said that Jesus could have all the kingdoms on earth if he worshipped the devil. But Jesus told him to go away, because the scriptures say that we should worship only God. After this, the devil left him alone.

Looking at this story, we see that Jesus was tempted to do things that he shouldn't, just as we are. Because Jesus went through this and didn't cave in to the pressure, he can help us with the same kind of stuff. He wouldn't be able to advise us very well if he'd never experienced it. As the story of his temptation shows, if we soak ourselves in the Bible by reading it every day, we can use it to deal with the bad things in our lives. Also, if we rely fully on God, we will be protected from the devil and his temptations.

It's important to remember that simply being tempted (in other words, wanting to do something wrong) is not a sin, as Jesus himself was tempted. You don't need to feel guilty about wanting to do something wrong—as long as you don't actually do it. When you are faced with temptation, it's better to avoid focusing on whatever is tempting you and focus on something positive instead, like God's love for you. Pray about the situation. It may be hard to admit to God what you're struggling with, but he knows about it anyway, so tell him all about it and ask him to help you through it.

Jesus says that if something is causing you to sin, you should get rid of it so that it is not a temptation to you (see Matthew 5:29). For example, if you are tempted to eat a box of chocolates that belongs to someone else, it's best to move the chocolates to another room or to leave the room yourself so that you can no longer see them. Sometimes, getting rid of the temptation is a lot harder to do, though. You may have a friend or a boyfriend who is putting pressure on you to do the wrong thing. Ask God to help you to know what to do and trust that he will lead you in the right direction.

Going back to the chocolates, if you give in to the temptation and eat them, you may feel good while you're eating them but afterwards you'll feel bad, so you'll end up worse off than when you started. Of course, God forgives us when we mess up, but we still have to try to avoid doing wrong, because bad stuff can get in the way of our relationship with God. And if our relationship with God is blocked, we can't listen to him as well as we should, so we will be more likely to feel stuck in our lives and in our faith.

Try to share what's tempting you with a friend. Tell them the problem and they may be able to help you through it, take your mind off it and remind you not to do it. Try not to feel ashamed or embarrassed that you're having problems, as everyone is tempted at some time, whether it's with food, alcohol, sex or something else. Even if you think you are strong enough not to give in to something that tempts you, be very careful!

Lord God, please show me the things that you wouldn't want me to do and help me to resist them. Please help me to be strong and help me to rely on you in difficult times. Help me to focus on you and to take time to read the Bible every day so that I can be made strong to fight against temptation. Help me to be able to talk to you, and others, about these things without being ashamed. Thank you for always listening. Amen

✳ To remember

If you stop sinning and start doing right, you will keep living and be secure for ever.

PSALM 37:27

✳ Reflection

- Think about what you're tempted to do. Why do you think God doesn't want you to do it?
- What are the pros and cons of giving in to this temptation?
- Are there people, places or objects in your life that add to the temptation? How can you prevent this from happening?

When you're being made fun of

What the Bible says

For all who are ill-treated, the Lord brings justice.

PSALM 103:6

Lord God, people are making fun of me and it's making me really upset. Please be with me and help me to get through it. Please comfort me and help me to know where to turn. Lord, I love you; please strengthen me to be able to stand up for you, even when it's difficult. Amen

When people are making fun of you because of what you believe, you may feel very alone, but you're not. Throughout the Bible we read of people being discriminated against for many different reasons, especially their faith. In 1 Peter 3:9–17, Peter tells us not to be nasty to people just because they're being nasty to us. He tells us to treat everyone with kindness and explains that, because God has chosen us, he will bless us, even if we have to suffer for doing good things. So we should stop worrying about what others will do to us and focus instead on honouring Jesus and making him the Lord of our life.

He goes on to say that we should always answer people kindly and truthfully when they ask us about what we believe, so that we can keep a clear conscience. If we don't counterattack, people may start to feel bad about the hurtful things they've said about us. After all, we've been doing good, not bad, by being a Christian. Peter finishes by saying that we are better off obeying God and suffering for doing right than suffering for doing wrong.

While Peter was talking to the early Christians who were hated because of their beliefs, what he said applies to anybody who is made fun of. It just goes to show that even 2000 years ago the same thing was happening, so you are definitely not alone. Wherever there is someone who is different in some way, people will tend to tease them, laugh at them and pick on them just because they are not the same as themselves.

Try not to get too upset about it and don't take it too personally. Quite often, people make fun of something just because they don't understand it or they don't quite know how to react. So they might not intend their teasing to be taken as nastiness. This is especially true if they are picking on you for your faith, as that is something a lot of people nowadays don't understand at all.

Think about it, though. If you're a Christian, what is it that makes you different? You're saved, you've got eternal life and you know where you're going! So next time people laugh at you for what you believe, just remember what it is that they're actually joking about and let it bounce off you.

Only the other day, I was in a church service where we all reflected on a worship song that said something about wanting to hide in God. This really struck me, as I always find myself wanting to run and hide away from difficulties. The song shows that it's actually fine to do this with God: if we trust in him and go to him when we are in trouble, he will protect us and form a barrier for us. He will bear insults for us and look after us. At the same time, we shouldn't spend our whole lives hiding behind God—we need to live out in the rest of the world, too.

In Matthew 27:44 we read that the two criminals who were crucified alongside Jesus joined in insulting him like all the others standing around. This reminds us how much Jesus suffered: people were so cruel to him that they wanted to kill him and let a convicted criminal go free in his place (see Matthew 27:15–26). Not only do we have a God who loves us, cares for us, listens to us and helps us, but he has also suffered cruelty. He understands, better than we can ever imagine, what it's like to be mocked for who you are, what you do and what you believe.

However, if you're being bullied and it's worse than a few comments every now and then, you do need to speak to someone about it, because that sort of thing should not go on. Whether it's happening at school, college, work or wherever, go and speak to a member of staff, a parent or a trusted friend. Anybody sympathetic will do. Explain the situation to them, ask them for advice, and they should be able to start sorting it out for you.

Speak to God about it, too. Jesus tells us that we should love our enemies (Luke 6:27), which is an incredibly hard thing to do. Next time someone says something nasty about you, try praying for them instead of hoping that something horrifically embarrassing happens to them as payback. Ask God to look after them and help them through whatever problems they've got. That way, you won't turn bitter towards them, as bitterness will only eat you up inside. Remember, it is often true that those who feel the need to gossip or make fun of others feel insecure themselves.

Dear Lord, when people make fun of me, it's so difficult to stay true to who I am. Please be with me and help me not to want to change myself because of what others think of me. Lord, I'm sorry if I've ever neglected you when people made fun of me, instead of running to hide in you; please help me not to do this in future. Help me to forgive those who are nasty to me and to pray for them rather than wishing them ill. Amen

✳ To remember

> Ask God to bless everyone who ill-treats you. Ask him to bless them and not to curse them.

> **ROMANS 12:14**

✳ Reflection

- What positive aspects of your life could result in people making fun of you because they don't understand or are jealous?
- How can you focus on this positive aspect and prove to others

that it's a good thing, not something to be ashamed of or to hide?

- How can you make it easier for yourself to forgive and pray for people who are nasty to you, rather than wishing bad things for them?

When you're angry

What the Bible says

Hatred stirs up trouble; love overlooks the wrongs that others do.

PROVERBS 10:12

Heavenly Father, I feel angry right now because of [what has happened]. Please be with me and calm my temper so that I can do what you want me to do, Lord. Please help me to show others love, even when I'm angry, as that is what I would want them to do to me. Help me to remember that it might not be their fault that I am feeling this way. Thank you for being with me. Amen

The book of Nehemiah tells us about a man called Nehemiah, who went back to Jerusalem from exile in a faraway land to help the people rebuild the huge city walls. In chapter 5, some of the people started complaining about the lack of food and money and about being ill-treated by those in authority. When Nehemiah heard, he became angry and went to the leaders, asking them how they could have done these things. He called a meeting to accuse the leaders of everything they had done wrong, which left them speechless (v. 8).

Nehemiah went on to tell the leaders that they should honour God in the way they lived so that people who held different beliefs couldn't find fault with them. He said that they should undo all the wrong that they had done, and they agreed to this (v. 12).

This story shows that being angry is not necessarily a bad thing, as Nehemiah's anger meant that he sorted out the problems the people were having. Often God stirs up anger in us when we're faced with injustice of some kind, so that we are moved to do something about it. We can also see that anger itself is not a sin

41

because Jesus himself got angry. It's how we respond to our anger that determines whether we get ourselves into trouble or not.

Matthew 21:12–13 tells how Jesus went into the temple and found people selling stuff in there. He got angry because this went against what God wanted, so he knocked over all the tables. If you see something wrong and get angry about it, that's OK as long as you do what's right as a result. For example, if you see someone being picked on, it's OK to get angry about it as long as you use that anger to help the other person in a constructive way. So, if your anger causes you to go to someone to get help for the person being bullied, that's good; but if it causes you to throw a punch at the bully yourself, it won't help because you'll just get drawn in to the argument, too.

It's when anger causes us to do wrong to others that it's a problem. If someone's done something that has really annoyed us, we naturally want to get our own back to get revenge on them. However, as I've mentioned before, Jesus teaches us to love our enemies, so next time someone gets you angry, try to stay calm about it. Take some deep breaths and think about God—that he loves you and he's there in the situation with you. If you can, take a minute or two out to read something in the Bible to calm you. Pray for the annoying person, asking God to bless them, as that can help to defuse anger.

Sometimes a situation gets us angry—for example, if our parents make us visit boring Great-Auntie Mabel instead of going to a party that we'd been looking forward to for ages. Try not to get stressed about it, but think about it from your parents' perspective. They are concerned for a lonely old lady who might not be around much longer, whereas you'll get plenty of opportunities to go to parties. You never know, Auntie Mabel may have her friend's good-looking grandson visiting! The same goes if it's a person who has annoyed us: be calm and try to take some time out to destress. Pray that something good will come out of the situation instead and you might be surprised about what actually happens.

Anger can turn into a big problem, though, and it can lead to all sorts of trouble. If you know that you have a quick temper and are prone to flare-ups, learn to recognise the signs in yourself and take positive steps to stop them escalating into uncontrolled anger. Whenever I'm in school, I wear a WWJD (What Would Jesus Do?) wristband so that if people irritate me I'm reminded to think about Jesus and how he would treat them. I'm sure he'd treat them very differently from my initial reaction.

If there's an issue that gets you angry often, even when you just think of it, try to talk to somebody about it. I know I say that about a lot of things, but it's amazing how much it does help: Jesus calls us to belong to the family of the Church for a reason. Find an adult whom you trust and just explain the situation to them. Simply getting it off your chest should help. Try not to stir up more trouble by blaming your anger purely on other people, though. If you don't feel comfortable talking it through, then write it down, maybe as a letter to God, and ask him to bring healing to the situation.

Lord God, I'm sorry for thinking negatively about people when I'm angry, and I'm sorry for the times when I do wrong or want to get revenge because of my anger. Lord, please be with me and help me not to do this. Help me to pray for these situations instead of feeling angry about them. When I get angry about some kind of injustice, though, please show me what I can do to help. Amen

☀ To remember

Don't get so angry that you sin. Don't go to bed angry and don't give the devil a chance.

EPHESIANS 4:26–27

☀ Reflection

• Think about what gets you angry. What exactly makes you feel that way?

- Can you think of a situation that you've been angry about, where something good has happened as a result?
- Why do you think Ephesians 4:27 says that getting angry gives the devil a chance?

When you're working for a good cause

What the Bible says

'Whenever you did [a good deed] for any of my people, no matter how unimportant they seemed, you did it for me.'

MATTHEW 25:40

Heavenly Father, when we feel enthusiastic about a good cause, please help us to keep that enthusiasm going and spread it to others so that many people will start wanting to do good things. Lord, please show us how we can take positive action to change our world for the better. Thank you for everything you've given us and for all the opportunities we have. Amen

Moses worked really hard for a great cause—leading the Israelites away from slavery in Egypt. In Exodus 4:10–17, though, when God first asks him to do that job, he starts to complain to God, saying that he is the wrong person to be a leader because he isn't very good at speaking to people. God replies that it was him who gave Moses his mouth, so he will give Moses the right words to say.

Moses still says that he can't do it, however, and begs God to ask someone else, to which God replies that Moses' brother Aaron is already on his way to meet him. He says that Aaron is a good speaker and that Moses should tell him what to say so that Aaron can speak for him. God also says that he will help them both to know what to say and will teach them what to do.

I find this story so encouraging as it shows that even Moses, one of the best-known people in the whole Bible, worried he wasn't good enough. It also shows that, despite his worries, he did prove good enough, as God helped him and guided him every step of the way. Even when Moses protests that he can't do it, God is one step ahead of him, as he has already sent Aaron to help him out.

This is a lot like us; we shouldn't be discouraged if we don't think we're good enough to lead people or organise something because, if it's what God is calling us to do, he will make sure we can do it and he will be with us the whole time. If there's something that we really can't do, well, God knows about that too and he will have already planned for someone else to take over.

I don't know about you, but every now and then some cause or charity will spark something off inside me and I'll desperately want to help. While giving some money is an obvious response, it is easy to forget that God may be calling us to get more directly involved.

Working for good causes by organising or helping at an event can have many positive repercussions, some of which you wouldn't even have considered. OK, the cause you're working for will benefit because you'll raise awareness, money or help for that cause, but there may be other ways in which you are helping, such as encouraging people closer to home to take a cause more seriously.

There are other, more unexpected benefits as well. For example, our youth group organised a quiz to raise money for a charity that campaigns against people-trafficking. In doing so, we raised awareness that this form of slavery is still going on, and we gave people in the local area a nice evening out. By doing the organising, though, we also became much closer friends as a group, because of the teamwork involved.

If you are a Christian and you organise a fund-raising event with your church for the cause, you may let others see how great Christianity is because of the fun you all have together. Depending on what you do, you can also make loads of friends and mix with lots of different people.

When a cause does fire up something within you, don't let that fire go out: nurture it, pray about it and ask God for guidance, showing you what you can do. Talk to others about it and try to get as many other people as possible interested. You might feel as if you're not the right person to get really involved, but, if God calls you by making you passionate about a cause, then you can do it.

You might not be sure if it is God calling you towards something or if it is just your imagination, but don't worry about it. If the cause that you're passionate about is a good one, if it will help people and you just can't shake it off, then the chances are that the inspiration does come from God.

It might be an environmental issue that you're concerned about, such as pollution or global warming. If this is the case, there are many steps that you can take yourself—even small ones such as turning unwanted lights off or recycling. Try to encourage your friends to take the same small steps as yourself and, if you feel brave enough, speak out about it at school or in church. If you do things like this, your little steps will add up to a huge step in the right direction.

Use whatever gifts you have in working for the cause, as God has given you those abilities for a reason. If you're really good at writing, write pamphlets, letters or a blog about what you're doing. If you're good at art, make some posters—there's tons of stuff you can do, no matter what you're good at. If you're organising an event, split the jobs up between different people, as there'll be enough to keep everyone busy. Don't forget to pray about it so that God can show you the best path to take.

Finally, don't let people put you off just because you're young. We might be young now, but it's our world, too, and we're the next generation. It's up to us to do something about issues such as caring for the environment, helping people who are suffering and putting a stop to cruelty.

Lord God, please fire us up with enthusiasm for good causes and show us how we can actively seek to change our world for the better. Thank you for the gifts that you've given us. I pray that we come to recognise those gifts and that you will show us how to use them for you. Help us not to give up and continue to encourage us. Amen

✳ To remember

If you do what the Lord wants, he will make certain each step you take is sure.

PSALM 37:23

✳ Reflection

- What aspects of a given cause have made you enthusiastic to help?
- What, realistically, could you do to raise money or awareness for this cause?
- What gifts have you been blessed with, through which you could contribute something?
- Who else might you end up helping if you organise an event?

When you're jealous of someone

What the Bible says

It's much better to be wise and sensible than to be rich.

PROVERBS 16:16

Dear Lord, when I'm feeling jealous, help me not to focus on those negative emotions. Please help me to feel pleased for [the person] instead of jealous and not to hold against them who they are, what they do or what they have. Lord, please help me to remember that you are the most important thing. Amen

James, one of Jesus' brothers, wrote a letter to help those trying to establish the church after Jesus' death. In James 2:1–4, he tells us that if we have faith in Jesus we won't treat some people better than others. He says that if a rich person comes to a church meeting wearing nice clothes and a poor person in ragged clothes also comes along, we shouldn't give the best seat to the rich person and make the poor person sit on the floor. He says that this is the same as saying that some people are better than others, which would make us like a really unfair judge.

God won't think any more or less of us because of what we own or how good we are at passing exams. Therefore, we should try not to be jealous of other people—such differences don't matter to God, and we should model ourselves on him. It's natural to be concerned about how others perceive us, but we should try not to let it rule our lives, as we can start feeling down because we can never keep up with their expectations. It's thoughts such as these that lead to jealousy.

In the Gospels, Jesus constantly reminds us that some things (such as love and friendship) are far more important than material possessions. In Luke 12:16–20 he tells the story of a stupid rich man who had so much stuff that he didn't have anywhere to put it. Instead of sharing it and enjoying what he had, he knocked down his barns to build himself even more storage space. Then he died and it all went to waste.

Because of this, Jesus reminds us to enjoy our time here while we have it, rather than worrying about earning loads of money or having tons of possessions and envying other people. If we stop worrying about material things, we'll end up much happier because we'll have time and energy to enjoy having a laugh with our friends and to celebrate who we are and what we have.

We all see people with stuff that we wish we had, and we all get jealous from time to time because someone, say, gets the grades we think we should have got, gets a pay rise when we feel we deserve one, gets a boyfriend when we'd love to go out with him—the list is endless. What's important is not to let the jealousy take over our lives, as only badness can come of that.

This can be difficult, especially when a situation seems really unfair, but that's just how life goes sometimes, horrible as it is. We know that God will be the ultimate judge. When we do something good that we don't get recognition for, he will always take note. In Matthew 6:3–4 we read that Jesus said, 'When you give to the poor, don't let anyone know about it. Then your gift will be given in secret. Your Father knows what is done in secret, and he will reward you.' God will notice, even if no one else does.

If we allow jealousy to grow inside us, it will cause us harm. Think about it: if you are jealous of someone and think bad things about them, will that person even be aware of it? In fact, the negative emotion will just live in your heart and eat up all your good feelings, because you won't be able to focus on them. You are the only person who will suffer because of it.

Instead, try to focus on the great stuff that you do have, such as (if you're a Christian) a relationship with God. Chances are there's something you have, whether it's part of your physical appearance or really good friends, that someone else wishes they had. Just remember that when you get to heaven, none of this will matter anyway—all material things will be changed and everyone will be equal.

Pray about it. When there's someone you feel really jealous of, try talking to God. He'll listen to you and comfort you. You could try being pleased for the other person, difficult though it may be—and remember that in the long term it won't matter anyway. If you pray for good things to happen to this person, you can find your negative feelings becoming positive ones.

Heavenly Father, please help me to realise that having lots of material possessions is not what is most important in life. Please help me to be grateful for what I have, instead of focusing on what I don't have. Lord, I thank you for the best thing of all, the fact that you sent your Son Jesus to die for us, so that every one of us can be forgiven. Amen

☀ To remember

Wisdom is worth more than silver; it makes you much richer than gold.

PROVERBS 3:14

☀ Reflection

- Why are you jealous of this person? How much happier would you really be if you had what they have?
- What gifts, abilities or possessions do you have that others might envy?
- What positive things can you pray for the person you're jealous of?

When you're scared

What the Bible says

'Don't be afraid! ... I will be with you and bless you.'

GENESIS 26:24

Dear Lord, I'm scared, please help me! The fear is taking me over and I don't know what to do. Please be with me and comfort me; allow me to get the strength I need from you. Please, Lord, help me to remember that you are on my side and that you can do anything. I know I can get through this with your love. Thank you, Lord. Amen

We have already thought about how Nehemiah tried to rebuild the wall of Jerusalem to give his people somewhere safe to live. In chapter 6 we read about all the opposition to his plans. Nehemiah's enemies sent him a letter saying that they wanted to meet him, but Nehemiah knew that they were planning to harm him, so he replied that he couldn't leave the wall while he was still working on it (v. 3).

The enemies kept saying that they wanted to meet him, until, on their fifth attempt to persuade him, they sent a letter accusing Nehemiah's helpers of planning to rebel against their rulers (v. 6). To this Nehemiah replied that his enemies were just inventing this story and were simply trying to frighten the people so that they would become too weak and discouraged to work and would not finish the wall. Nehemiah prayed that God would strengthen him.

These verses show that people who are opposed to what we're doing will often try to frighten us into failing. This is especially true if we're doing something for God, as the enemy will try to make us feel as if we simply can't do the job, or that something bad will happen as a result of it, to try to put us off.

When we feel scared, the fear can seem to take over so that we can't even manage simple things properly. We panic, our pulses race, we rush through every possibility in our minds and we know that there's nothing we can do about the situation. OK, stop there. There might be nothing that we can do, but what if we had someone on our side who could do absolutely everything? From solving the problem itself to simply calming us down, there is nothing that God cannot do, and he is on our side.

Because of this fact, there actually is something we can do: we can pray. God may not take away the problem, but talking it through with him will certainly make us feel better and will show us how to handle it. We should also remember that, although we're scared now, we could learn from our difficulties and become stronger people in the future.

One of the hardest things to do when you're scared is to use your common sense, but this is probably the most helpful thing to do. Think about the situation logically. Perhaps you're scared because you're at home by yourself in the dark. Tell yourself what those creepy shadows really are and actively stop your imagination from drawing vivid pictures of flesh-eating monsters, which, let's face it, are not going to be lurking in your bathroom. Instead, focus on something that's real and positive. It could simply be a good programme on the TV or ringing up a friend for a chat.

Think about the worst that can happen. Your mind may come up with the picture of some gory way that you could die by, say, tripping over a rug, but try not to dwell on these thoughts. Are they really likely to happen? Instead, think about the worst that is actually likely to happen. Chances are, it's not going to be so bad after all. If you are at home alone, the worst thing that's likely to happen could be that there won't be anything worth watching on TV.

When you are scared, it's important to be calm so that you don't end up a nervous wreck. Stop whatever you're doing and take a few deep breaths. Close your eyes for a few seconds and try to fill your insides with calm. Pray that God will fill you with his peace. Remember, God is always with you, so you don't ever need to feel that you're alone.

Lord God, I pray that you will be with me now, because I'm scared. Please help me to feel your presence and be comforted by it. When I'm scared, please help me to remember to pray and to know that you are close by me, because you can help me through anything. Amen.

※ To remember

I asked the Lord for help, and he saved me from all my fears.

PSALM 34:4

※ Reflection

- Think about what you're scared of. Can you identify the specific aspect of it that scares you?
- What is the worst thing, logically, that could happen to you? Does this make your fear seem rational?
- How can you grow as a person or in your faith by not letting this fear get the better of you?

When you're anxious about the future

What the Bible says

We make our own plans, but the Lord decides where we will go.

PROVERBS 16:9

Father, I'm really anxious about the future because I just don't know what's going to happen. Please help me to trust in you because you know everything. Please lead me on the right path so that I end up doing what's right for me and, in the meantime, please ease my worries and help me to feel secure. Thank you for always being there for me. Amen

In the book of Acts, a load of Jesus' disciples went around sharing his teaching, as Jesus was no longer with them. Acts 14:8–10 tells the story of a man who had crippled feet. He'd been born that way and had never been able to walk. One day, he was listening to Paul speaking and Paul saw that he had faith in Jesus. Because of this, Paul looked straight at the man and shouted to him to stand up. The man did—in fact, he jumped up and started walking about.

Because this man believed in Jesus, he was able to stand up, even though, for his whole life, he'd believed that he couldn't. It is exactly the same for you. You may have believed for your whole life that you couldn't possibly do something, but, if you put your trust in Jesus, then you will be able to. The Bible says that God has a plan for all of us. As Jeremiah 29:11 says, 'I will bless you with a future filled with hope—a future of success, not of suffering.' That future might be something that you'd never even thought about, but God knows what's right and he will let it happen at the right time.

The future can still be a really scary prospect: there seem to be so many decisions to make. What subjects to study, whether or not to stay on at school, what job to go for, which universities to apply for, what career you're interested in—and all of that is just to do with work. There are tons of other choices, too, but it's reassuring to remember that absolutely everybody has to make them, in one way or another.

Everyone panics about the future at some point and loads of people have no idea what career they want while they're still teenagers or even beyond—including people who later become really successful. We should remember that, whatever we do in the future, the one constant will be God—his love for us does not change.

For me, one of the best things about being a Christian is that I know God has plans for each and every one of us; even though we may feel totally aimless, we are actually heading in some sort of direction. We may feel that we can't cope with the uncertainty of the future and we can't make decisions, but that's OK because God will lead us in the right direction.

Just pray to God and ask him to show you the way to go and reassure you when you are feeling worried. Obviously, though, you have to make your own choices and no one can force you to do anything—including God. That's why he gave us free will, so we can make decisions and do what we want to do. The thing is, though, that if we follow God's way, then life will be a hundred times more satisfying than if we try to go it alone.

It can be hard to know what exactly God is calling us to do, as he doesn't lasso us with the Holy Spirit, drag us to the door of an office and float an application form into our hands. If you are passionate about something and good at it, whether it's horse riding or art, God is the one who created you with those gifts and interests, so it's likely that that's the path he's prepared for you.

Don't worry too much about making the wrong decision—if something really doesn't feel right, it's rarely too late to change your mind. Just pray to God at every step of the way so that he can guide you, and he'll give you all the second (and third, fourth and millionth) chances you need.

Talk to people you know, as well. Anybody who's older and more experienced will be able to offer advice. They can't tell you what to do, but they can reassure you and help you to find your own way.

Dear God, please be with me throughout my future and help me not to stray from you. When I go through difficult times, please help me to remember to rely on you. Please, Lord, help me keep up a strong relationship with you because then I can be sure that nothing in the future can trouble me, because you will protect me. Thank you, Lord. Amen

❋ To remember

His glorious power will make you patient and strong enough to endure anything, and you will be truly happy.

COLOSSIANS 1:11

❋ Reflection

- What are you enthusiastic about? How could you involve those passions in your future plans?
- How many people do you know who have always known exactly what they wanted to do?
- Think of something you were sure you could never do, such as difficult maths problems or going to interviews, that you later learned to do. What does that teach you for the future?

When you're not getting on with someone

What the Bible says

Put up with each other, and forgive anyone who does you wrong, just as Christ has forgiven you.

COLOSSIANS 3:13

Lord God, please help me to be patient when I find people irritating. Help me, too, to forget the past when I've had an argument with somebody. Help me to forgive people after we've had a fight, because you always forgive me when I do something wrong. Thank you, Lord. Amen

In the first book of Samuel, God tells David that he will defeat all his enemies and become great. In chapter 24, King Saul goes into a cave after leading his army in battle against another nation. David is hiding at the back of the cave with his men and knows that if he kills Saul there and then, he could become the next king. So he sneaks up behind Saul, but all he does is cut off a piece of Saul's robe (v. 4).

Afterwards David feels bad about doing even this. He tells his men that they shouldn't be so stupid as to kill the king, and he prays that God will help him not to harm Saul (v. 6). Saul leaves the cave, but David chases after him and shows him the piece of cloth that he has cut off. He tells Saul that he had the opportunity to kill him, but held back. Saul is really grateful for this (as you'd expect!) and tells David that he's done the right thing and that he will certainly become the next king.

Even though David and Saul were enemies, when David had the chance to harm Saul, he didn't, and found that he was really glad about it. When Saul realised how kind David had been to him by sparing his life, he gave him his blessing, something that could never have happened if David had killed him in the first place. This shows that if we do the right thing rather than acting on our impulses when we want to do someone harm, more good can come of it than we could ever have imagined.

This doesn't just apply to wanting to kill someone so that you can get their power, which sounds far too Shakespearean to relate to most people's lives. The same applies if you want to spread rumours about someone because they've stolen your friends or if you want to shout at your sister for borrowing your favourite top without asking. Try to hold back and you'll be surprised at what good can result.

OK, some people are just hard to get on with, no matter what you do. It's best to try to be patient and, if you think you're going to do or say something that you could regret, just walk away. You can even try to do that in a nice way. Go off to the toilet or something, simply so that you can get a break from the situation. Ask God for the patience you need.

It's the same if you fall out with someone close to you, whether you've had an argument or whatever. Just stay calm and try to be patient with them. Yes, it's really hard but, again, ask God to help you. If someone's done something to upset you, you have to forgive them—even if you're convinced they don't deserve it.

That can be one of the hardest parts of being a Christian. But think about it: if you'd done something wrong to your friends, you'd want them to forgive you, wouldn't you? What if there was somebody who cared about you more than you could possibly imagine and you kept on doing hurtful things to them? Do you think they'd forgive you? Well, both of those examples apply to God, and yes, he does forgive you, every single time you act against him.

So try to forgive and forget when you fall out with someone; try not to provoke an argument; try to be patient when somebody's being annoying. Those three things may seem hard but you've got God behind you the whole way. Pray for the people you can't get on with, so that God will bless them. If you do that, they may become happier or, at least, less difficult as far as you're concerned.

When you've truly forgiven someone, that's it. You don't keep reminding them of what they've done and you don't hold a grudge against them for eternity, because grudges will just eat you up inside. That's why it is so difficult to forgive someone wholeheartedly, but you can do it. When they say nasty or annoying stuff, try to 'turn the other cheek', as Jesus put it (Matthew 5:39)—ignore their unkindness and say kind words in return. They'll soon get fed up because they can't provoke you, and you can hold your head up high because you know you've done what's right.

Dear Lord, someone's done something that has really upset me. I don't want to forgive them, but please help me to be able to do that, Lord. Please heal the emotional wounds between us and help us to become friends again. Lord, please help me not to hold a grudge against them but to be able to forgive and forget, just as you do. Amen

❋ To remember

'Love your enemies and pray for anyone who ill-treats you.'

MATTHEW 5:44

❋ Reflection

- If you're finding someone irritating, try to work out exactly what it is about them that annoys you. How can you try to overlook it?
- If you've fallen out with someone, how can you approach them to let them know that you're sorry and want to forgive them?
- What could happen if you both managed to put the past behind you and started to get on well?

When you're working

What the Bible says

Anyone who can be trusted in little matters can also be trusted in important matters. But anyone who is dishonest in little matters will be dishonest in important matters.

LUKE 16:10

Dear God, please help me when I find it hard to keep going with the work that I have to do. When I find it boring, please reassure me that I am in the right place and, when I find it difficult, please show me how to get the help I need. Please encourage me in my work, Lord, and help me to do what's right. Amen

The book of 2 Thessalonians is the second letter by Paul, the inspiring leader of the early Church, to the Christians in Thessalonica. In chapter 3 and verses 6–13 he advises the people not to be lazy. He says that they should avoid people who waste time and don't follow instructions and, instead, follow the example that he himself set.

Paul states that he and the people working with him didn't waste time and always paid for any food they were given. They worked hard so that they wouldn't burden anyone and so that they could set a good example of Christian behaviour. However, Paul says that he has heard about some of the Thessalonians wasting time and refusing to work. He begs them to settle down and start pulling their weight. He finishes by saying that they should never get tired of doing the right thing.

And that is exactly what you and I should do! It sounds like a lot of hard work to always do what's right and work as hard as we can, but that's what we have to aim for. It doesn't matter if we're not perfect all of the time because, let's face it, we are only human—

but we have to try. Whether it's homework, coursework, revision or paid work, none of us can escape doing work of some kind and at times it can be pretty stressful. Sometimes it just seems boring and we don't want to do it. Sometimes we can't get motivated to do what we ought to do and at other times it seems too difficult.

In any of these cases, it's important to think about why you're doing this work. If it's any kind of schoolwork, you're doing it so that you can earn the qualifications you need to get a job in the future—something that God has called you to or you're passionate about (and, as we've seen, those can be the same thing). If you're doing paid work, then money will probably be the main factor, but experience is also important. Try to focus on your reasons for being there and then the negative stuff won't seem so unbearable.

In any kind of work, we can try to dedicate it to God. This might sound a bit strange, but give it a go. We can imagine that everything we're doing is for God. For a short time, I had a Saturday job in a supermarket, which I really didn't like because it was so boring. Yet someone told me to dedicate it to God, so I tried to do my absolute best as if I was stacking the shelves for God. The time ended up going much faster because I was putting so much effort in, and I enjoyed it a lot more because I felt that I was really doing my best. My supervisors noticed how well I was doing, too.

When we're working, it's important to know when to stop and rest. If we find ourselves hating our work, whatever it is, it's quite often because we're tired. Apparently, the brain stops taking in information after about 20 or 30 minutes when we're studying. So, if you're doing revision, you need to make sure you keep taking breaks so that your brain can continue to focus.

If you're working at a job, you'll get a break every few hours or so anyway, so make sure you make the most of those breaks. Take a book and sit somewhere peaceful with it, even if you don't actually read it—it'll give you an excuse to sit quietly for a while. Spend some time with God, because he'll refresh you and give you the peace you need.

It's also important to know when to say 'no'. If you are being asked to do more and more shifts, you should make sure you turn them down every now and then so that you can give yourself the rest that you need.

If you are doing paid work, you might feel that you need to work as much as you can because you need the money, which can make you more stressed and tired than ever. Try to relax and not worry about it so much. If you need the money badly, pray to God about it, because he has promised that he'll provide us with everything we need (Matthew 6:31–32). However, if you just want the money for extra shopping, try to remember that fashionable clothes aren't everything. What's more important is making sure that your well-being is—well, well! So take the time off if you need it.

Even if the work you're doing seems completely pointless now, remember that once you've got those qualifications or that experience, God will be able to use them to shape your life in a much more purposeful way.

Lord God, please be with me when I'm working and help me to be able to enjoy it in whatever way I can. Please help me to focus on the positive aspects so that the negatives don't seem so bad. Help me to know when I need a rest and give me the courage to say 'no' every now and then, so that I don't end up getting stressed. And, Lord, please help me to use my work to serve you and others in the best way possible. Amen

☀ To remember

Don't give up your job when your boss gets angry. If you stay calm, you'll be forgiven.

ECCLESIASTES 10:4

☀ Reflection

• What's the worst kind of work you've ever done? Why was it so bad?

- What's the best kind of work you've ever done? Why was it so good?
- Whether this work was paid work or schoolwork, how can you get those positive attributes into the difficult work that you may find yourself having to do?

When you feel stressed

What the Bible says

God's Spirit makes us loving, happy, peaceful, patient, kind, good, faithful, gentle and self-controlled.

GALATIANS 5:22–23

Father, right now I feel so stressed that I feel I can't cope with all I have to do. Lord, please help me to feel that you are with me, and help me to be strong so that I can get through this situation that I find so hard to face. Help me to find hope and wise advice in the pages of your word, the Bible. Thank you for being there for me—and for us all. Amen

In Exodus 18, Moses' father-in-law, Jethro, comes to visit him and finds out how much work Moses is doing to help everyone. In verses 18–23 he gives Moses some good advice. He says that Moses will soon be worn out, as the work is too much for one person and he can't do it alone. God will help him if he takes the following advice: he should appoint some leaders who respect God and are trustworthy and honest and then split them into groups. These groups should then deal with most of the work and only bring the difficult cases to Moses. Jethro says that having the other leaders to share the load will make Moses' work easier and that this is the way God wants it to be done. He finishes by saying that Moses won't be under as much stress and everyone will be left feeling satisfied.

That is such good advice, and it's so practical. It shows that God gives us the strength to cope with whatever we need to do, but, when we start to struggle, we should recognise it as a sign that we're taking too much on. That's when we need to try to turn down some responsibilities or get help to spread the workload. God knew that Moses was struggling so he sent Jethro along to give him the advice he needed.

When you're committed to lots of different projects, it can be easy to become stressed because you don't want to let anybody down. Schoolwork, exams, jobs and relationships can all make us feel stressed; it's all too common in today's world, where everyone is always rushing around.

Try to spread your time out evenly, so that you have some opportunity to rest, relax and have fun, as well as to do your work and see the people you need to see. Work out priorities: make a list of all your tasks and put them in order of importance. Then cross them off as you achieve each one. You'll be amazed at how good it feels! Don't expect to get everything done, but, if you start with the most important items, it won't matter so much if the last jobs on the list don't happen in the end.

One thing that can make us feel really stressed out is taking exams, but unfortunately everyone has to do them at some point. It's important not to panic, as that just makes you even more stressed. Make sure you're prepared: plan out all the topics you need to revise and start well in advance so that you don't have a mad rush at the last minute. Take plenty of breaks and make sure you get enough sleep, as that's far more helpful than late-night cramming. Pray about your exams and ask God to relax you. I find it really helpful to do this as soon as I've opened my exam paper so that he can clear my mind and help me to remember everything I've learnt.

Remember that everyone feels stressed from time to time, so you won't be exempt. It may be, though, that you feel stressed because you're working hard to meet the high expectations that you set for yourself. No one will mind if you hand in an essay that's below your usual standard every now and then (as long as it is only every now and then!) or if you turn down a shift at work. Your teachers or supervisors are more likely to moderate their expectations of you if you're honest with them about how you feel—so remember to be lenient on yourself, too.

I've found that when I'm feeling really stressed, the best thing to do is to stop and have some me-time. Stop completely, even if it's just for five minutes, and get yourself some peace and quiet. A lot of people think that they can't do this because they've simply got too much to do, but you will get much more done if you have a short break from time to time than if you force yourself to keep going.

When you're having this quiet moment, try to spend it with God, as that really helps. Read the Bible (or perhaps some of the Bible bits from this book), as it has lots of encouraging verses in it that can calm you and help you to avoid stress as much as possible. Spend some time in prayer or just rest in God's presence without saying anything at all. Try to feel him around you: this can sound a bit creepy if you haven't done it before, but it is actually very reassuring. It can be easy to forget that our God is a loving father, not a scowling head teacher waiting to get angry, so just relax in his presence and be ready for him to comfort you and give you the peace you need.

Dear Lord, when I am feeling tense, help me to remember that there is a time for everything and that I must take time out for rest, even when I feel as if I have far too much to do. Please be with me in my times of quiet and help me to sense your presence bringing me peace. Thank you for being with me, Lord. Amen

✳ To remember

'If you are tired from carrying heavy burdens, come to me and I will give you rest.'

MATTHEW 11:28

✳ Reflection

- Think about all the tasks you have to do. How many of them are actually necessary? You'll be surprised at how many you don't have to do right now.

- How can you break up your work to make the load more manageable? Who do you know who might be able to help you out? Pray about it—God will lead you in the right direction. (Make sure you make space to listen, though!)
- Sit in the quiet for a few minutes (even if that means simply locking yourself in a toilet) and close your eyes. Think about a really calm, relaxing place, such as a beach or a field—whatever works for you—and imagine being there and feeling the sun on your skin. Take slow, deep breaths until you feel calmer.

When you're going through a big change

What the Bible says

Though I live high above in the holy place, I am here to help those who are humble and depend only on me.

ISAIAH 57:15

Dear God, everything's changing and I find it both scary and exciting. Please be with me and help me to focus on the positives. Show me the right things to do and the right ways to act, so that I can do what you want me to do and stay close to you, even though everything feels different. Please comfort me and help me to know your peace at this difficult time. Amen

Throughout the Bible, we see people having to go through huge changes in their lives—and none more so than the disciples who left everything behind to go and follow Jesus. The story of the day when Jesus chose his first disciples is told in Luke 5:1–11. Jesus was teaching people by a lake, and there were some fishing boats on the shore. He got into Simon's boat and asked him to row it out into the water, from where Jesus continued to teach.

When he'd finished talking to the people, Jesus told Simon to row to the deep water to catch some fish. Simon replied that they'd been fishing all night and hadn't caught anything, but he would let the nets down anyway as Jesus had asked him to. He did so and caught so many fish that the nets started to rip.

The other fishermen came to help and were shocked at what had happened. Jesus told them not to be scared and that from now on they would bring in people instead of fish. So the fishermen pulled their boats on to the shore, left everything and went off with Jesus.

That must have been a huge decision for them to make—to forget about absolutely everything else and go with this man whom they hardly knew. Yet Jesus had shown them how powerful he was by performing the miracle of enabling them to catch tons of fish. They could trust his authority and know that he would look after them, even though their lives were being turned upside down.

When we're going through a big change, whether it's moving house, going to a new school, leaving for university or starting a new job—anything—it can be pretty scary because we don't know what to expect. Wouldn't it be great if we could go through it all with someone alongside us who knows exactly what's going to happen at every step of the way? Well, we can! God has everything planned for us, and his presence will always be with us. It says so all through the Bible, particularly in John 16:5–15, where Jesus tells us that his Spirit will always be with us.

When facing big changes, it's best not to focus so much on the little details that you don't know about—exactly what to do or where to go as soon as you arrive, stuff like that—because you're just not going to know until you actually get there. Instead, focus on the bigger picture—the general atmosphere that you're going into and the exciting new challenges that you're going to face, which will help you to grow in many different ways. If you keep worrying about the little things, you'll just end up going mad!

Just as when you're revising for an exam, you can make sure you're well prepared for the change. Find out as much as you can about the situation you're going into (there's bound to be stuff on the Internet), so that you have a general idea of what is likely to happen. Spend lots of time with God beforehand, praying and reading the Bible, so that you can build up your inner defences against discouragement and worry as the change unfolds.

Proverbs 2:10 says, 'Wisdom will control your mind, and you will be pleased with knowledge.' This is what can happen to us if we soak our minds in the words of the Bible, God's words to us. They will become second nature to us so that, when we're faced with a challenge, we'll be better equipped to deal with it. For example, if we're worrying about tomorrow, we can suddenly be reminded of

Jesus' words on worry in Matthew 6:25–34. Remember that, no matter what else is changing in your life, God's love is constant and it will not change, as Romans 8:38–39 reminds us.

If you're a Christian, remember that going through a big change can help you to grow in your faith, simply because it requires so much faith. You don't know exactly what's going to happen, so you have to trust in God more, which is the very basis of faith. If you're not a Christian, then a big change can still help you grow as a person, as you have to learn to cope on your own—but the key thing to believe is that you are not alone. God is with you and will protect you, whether you're aware of it or not. If you learn to trust him more, those huge unknown situations will start to seem less daunting.

Lord, please help me to trust you more and to know that you really will look after me through this time of change. Please fill me with peace and help me to be as prepared as possible. Lead me to Bible passages that will encourage me, and help me to remember them. When I face challenges that I don't know how to deal with, please give me strength to keep going and courage to try to sort things out in the right way. Thank you for always being with me, Lord. Amen

☀ To remember

'You will know that I stand at your side.'

JOEL 2:27

☀ Reflection

- What scares you about the change that you're going through? Who could you go to for advice about it?
- What do you find exciting about the change that you're going through? How can you make sure you get the best out of it?

- In what ways do you think you'll grow as a result of this experience?

When it's a special occasion

What the Bible says

Be joyful and sing as you come in to worship the Lord!

PSALM 100:2

Heavenly Father, I thank you for [this special occasion]. I thank you for the friends and family I can share it with and all the fun that we can have. Lord, thank you that you created everything, including all the reasons we have to celebrate. I thank you for the most special occasion of all, when you sent your Son to earth to die for us, because you love us so much. Amen

There are loads of special occasions in the Bible that people celebrated, but I think one of the most relevant to us is the Lord's Supper (see Luke 22:14–20), as we join in that celebration even today, in church Communion services. Jesus gathered all his disciples together and told them that he wanted to share the Passover meal (an annual Jewish celebration) with them before his time of suffering.

Jesus took some wine and thanked God for it, then told his disciples to share it among themselves. He took some bread, thanked God for that, too, broke it up and gave it to his disciples, telling them that it was his body, which he would sacrifice for them (v. 19). He told them that they should eat the bread and drink the wine—which was his blood, given for them—to remember him after he'd gone.

I think the fact that Jesus told his disciples how much he wanted to share the meal with them before he died shows us how important these friends were to Jesus. Perhaps he is reminding us that we too should take time out with our friends and family, even when other things seem more important. God will be in that time of relaxation.

It's amazing how often we forget about God on special occasions because we're so busy enjoying ourselves. It's important to take some time out to be with him, though, especially as it's because of him that most of these occasions happen! If you're celebrating Christmas or Easter, of course these times are all about God— celebrating Jesus' birth and his resurrection. Don't forget about that, just because the adverts tell you they're actually about presents, party clothes and chocolate eggs. If you're celebrating a birthday, remember that God is the one who invented birthdays. After all, he created birth and he formed each of us right from conception (Psalm 139:16).

Whatever the situation is, try not to forget about God in the middle of it all, because he wants to be your best friend, and you would hate it if your best friend didn't speak to you for days because he or she was off partying. It doesn't mean that you have to stop celebrating, just because you're spending some time with God. It should be the opposite: right through the Bible, God tells us to be joyful (see Isaiah 55:12–13, for example), so let him in on the celebration and he'll make you even happier.

If you're spending time with lots of people on this special occasion, try to get them all to remember Jesus at some point, too. If you're spending time with a bunch of Christians, this is easier because you can suggest saying a prayer together or something— perhaps grace before you eat. Of course it's harder if you're with people who have no interest in faith. If it's Christmas or Easter, though, why not simply drop a hint or two, just to make them think? They really shouldn't be opposed to that if they're happy to celebrate these occasions. You could say something simple, like, 'Isn't it amazing to think that we're celebrating Jesus being born/ resurrected today?'

Special occasions can be a great way of reaching people outside the church. For example, one Valentine's Day my boyfriend and I went to the church of a friend of ours, where they were having a party for the local community. They had big red hearts everywhere and candles and a buffet and dancing, but they also had a worship band and a short talk from their pastor about what love means. It was a really fun night, but it was also a chance to show that the church likes celebrating and that Jesus can be included in special occasions, too—even the ones that aren't centred on him.

Whatever the occasion is, have a great time! Jesus loved parties, and he was the best guest ever when he turned water into wine at a wedding (see John 2:1–11). If you know someone who will be spending a special occasion on their own, why not follow Jesus' example and invite them along to whatever you're doing? You could be surprised at the enjoyment they can add!

Dear God, without you we would have nothing to celebrate at all. Please help me not to forget this during special occasions, and help me sensitively to remind the people around me about you and your love as well. Please lead me to those who have to spend special occasions by themselves, and show me how to include them in the fun. Amen

❉ To remember

With thankful hearts, sing psalms, hymns, and spiritual songs to God. Whatever you say or do should be done in the name of the Lord Jesus, as you give thanks to God the Father because of him.

COLOSSIANS 3:16A–17

❉ Reflection

- What is the biggest thing that you have to celebrate at the moment? How does God tie into it?
- How can you bring God into the picture as you think about the celebrations for whatever special occasion you're having?

When you're worried about your appearance

What the Bible says

God loves you and has chosen you as his own special people.

COLOSSIANS 3:12

Dear Lord, sometimes I really hate how I look. Please comfort me and help me not to feel so useless. Help me to focus on the positives and not worry so much about the things I don't like about myself. Help me not to worry about what other people think of me and to remember that you love me just as I am. Amen

The Psalms are full of people enthusing about how wonderful God is (in the form of poetry—it's not just rambling!) and loads of them are really helpful and comforting. Psalm 139, written by King David, tells us that God is always near and that he looks deep into our hearts and knows all about us, including all our thoughts. He knows what we'll say before we speak and he protects us completely. There is no place on earth where we could escape God's Spirit. Even if we travel to the other side of the world, God will protect us.

The psalm says that God is the one who put us together before we were born and that everything God does is fantastic. Absolutely nothing about us is hidden from him and he is always at our side.

I find those verses really comforting as they show that we don't have to be ashamed about anything. God knows everything about us anyway and even created us. He planned everything about us from before we were born, and he will protect us from everything.

So when you find yourself wishing you were slimmer or had shinier hair, just remember that God thinks you're special, no matter what anyone else thinks—including yourself. Most of the time, we're our own worst critics. I mean, who else is going to stand in front of you scrutinising your face and pointing out your spots? Chances are, no one else will even notice whatever it is you're worrying about. How often do you look at someone and think 'Her nose is so humungous!' or 'How ugly is she?' You just don't! So other people won't be spending time thinking those things about you.

Try not to worry too much what others think of you, anyway. Yes, it's hard, especially when you want people to like you, but all you can do is be yourself. They're going to like you much more for being relaxed and fun than for staring in the mirror every ten seconds to see how big your bum looks or constantly dashing off to reapply your make-up.

Remember that God made you the way you are for a reason. You might not like the way you look but God does, because he thinks that all of us are really special. I know that sounds quite cheesy and American-feel-good-movie-ish, but it's true. You may think your ears are too big. Well, maybe God made you like that because one day you'll meet a wonderful man who loves big ears. That might sound strange, but I'm sure you get the idea...

God made us different because, if we were all the same, we'd just be weird clones and not proper humans. So if you diss the way you look, you're actually dissing God, because he's the one who made you that way. The Bible tells us that material things are not what's most important in life, because they just fade away (check out Matthew 6:19–21). What is important is stuff like good friends and a close relationship with God, so we should try to focus on those rather than on how good-looking we are (or not) compared with others.

Spending loads of time and effort dieting and buying posh clothes probably won't make you feel any better about yourself—you'll just end up hungry and broke! Look at the celebs who are always going on fad diets. Are most of them really happy? Of course, it's right to eat healthily and it's OK to make yourself feel good by treating yourself to new clothes. Just don't go over the top and let food or clothes dominate your life.

What can really make you feel better is developing your relationship with God. Spend time getting to know him through prayer and reading the Bible and you'll soon start to realise just how much someone very important cares about you. The Holy Spirit is the best natural high ever—most Christians will tell you that!

Heavenly Father, I thank you so much that you created me and that you care about me more than I can imagine. Help me to remember this and to focus on it when I'm feeling down. Help me, too, to appreciate the fact that you created me, especially when I worry about how I look. May I remember to spend more time with you so that I can feel good about myself, and may I know how special I am in your eyes. Amen

❋ To remember

God's love never fails.

PSALM 136:1B

❋ Reflection

- What do you think is your best feature?
- Do you think your good friends would like you any more if you looked different?
- If you could change one thing about your looks, what would it be and why? How happy would it make you?

When you want a boyfriend

What the Bible says

Your kindness and love will always be with me each day of my life, and I will live for ever in your house, Lord.

PSALM 23:6

Dear God, I haven't got a boyfriend and I feel so left out. Please comfort me and help me not to feel lonely, but to focus instead on all the good relationships that I do have. In your time, Lord, please lead me to the right person to be my boyfriend, and thank you that you always love me. Amen.

When the great early Church leader Paul wrote a letter to the Christians in Rome, he talked a lot about God's love for us, especially in Romans 8:31–39. Paul says, if God is on our side, how can anyone be against us? God proved that he is on our side by sending Jesus to die for us, so he will surely give us anything else we want. And if God says that we're acceptable to him, how can anyone else condemn us?

Paul says that nothing can separate us from the love God has for us: not trouble, suffering, hard times, hunger, nakedness, danger or death. He says that because of this we've won a victory, because not even life or death, angels or spirits, the present or future or powers above or below us can separate us from God's love.

Isn't it fantastic to think that there's someone out there, someone with all the power in the universe, who loves you and will never stop loving you, no matter what happens? Well, that's true and that's what Paul is going on about here. It gets a bit repetitive, but that's just because he's so astounded that God loves him so much.

We need to remember that even if we feel as if no boy in the universe is ever going to fancy us, God loves us and always will. Not having a boyfriend can seem really lonely; trust me, I've been there! Try not to worry about it too much, though, because if you look miserable all the time, it will be even harder for you to find one! Relax and enjoy being with your friends; the right guy will come along when the time is right—and that's important to remember, too. It might feel like the end of the world because all your friends have boyfriends and you don't, but in the long run it might turn out to be the best thing.

Perhaps it's actually best for you to get really close to your girlfriends before you get a boyfriend, so that they are there for you when you need them most. There could be a million and one different reasons why you don't have a boyfriend right now, but try to trust that God knows what's best for you, whether you believe it or not, and that his timing is perfect. The right person for you may be just around the corner.

You'll probably come across him when you least expect to, so make sure your eyes are open. Don't think that you have to have a particular 'type' as your boyfriend. The boy of your dreams could be standing right in front of you, but you haven't noticed because you always thought you'd like a blond. Pray about it and ask God to lead you in the right direction.

Remember that if you haven't got a boyfriend, it doesn't mean you're an ugly mutant blob who could never be attractive in a million years! As we have already seen, God made you and designed you even before you were born, so he thinks you're special, and he made you the way you are for a purpose, so that when the right guy comes along he will like you just for who you are.

You could try going out more to various places where you can meet lots of people, as that'll make it easier for you to find the right person. Whether it's going to different church events or hanging out with a bigger group of friends, the more people you meet, the more likely you are to find someone. Don't go for that reason alone, though, or you'll look a bit crazy, checking out all the boys for their potential. Just go to have fun! That special friendship will happen at the right time, even if it seems impossible at this moment. Pray about it—and pray for patience and hope.

At the time of writing, I've been with my boyfriend for over a year and a half. I met him at a Christian event that I nearly didn't go to because I didn't know anyone there. A friend had cancelled on me at the last minute, but if she had come with me I would never have started talking to Matt. So don't be afraid to go for something if you think God is pushing you towards it. You never know what could happen!

Lord God, please help me to be patient while I don't have a boyfriend, and lead me in the right direction so that I can find somebody who's right for me. Help me to be confident to be myself and to trust you. If it's not right for me at the moment, help me to accept that and please comfort me when I feel left out. Thank you for your love, Lord. Amen

☀ To remember

Learn to be patient, so that you will please God and be given what he has promised.

HEBREWS 10:36

☀ Reflection

- Why might it not be the best time for you to have a boyfriend right now?
- What are the positive qualities about yourself (especially your personality) that could be attractive to boys?
- What groups or activities could you get involved with, which would make it easier for you to meet new people?

When you're in love

What the Bible says

Love should be your guide.

I CORINTHIANS 14:1A

Lord God, I thank you so much for [this person] and for the love that we share. Lord, thank you that you created love, and please help me not to forget that. Thank you that you loved me so much that you died for me. Amen

1 Corinthians 13 is a famous chapter from Paul's first letter to the church at Corinth, in Greece. He starts by posing rhetorical questions, such as what would happen if he could speak every language; what if he could foretell the future; what if he could understand everything; what if he had faith that could move mountains; what if he gave away everything and was burned alive because of his faith in God? After each of these questions, he says that if he didn't love others, he would have nothing.

He then talks about love itself, saying that it is kind and patient, not jealous or boastful, proud or rude, that it isn't selfish or short-tempered and that it doesn't remember the mistakes that other people make. He says that love is truthful, supportive, loyal, hopeful and trusting. Love doesn't fail—it will last for ever! Even when prophecies stop being given, when languages stop being spoken and everything else is forgotten, love will still remain.

I find the first part of what Paul says here so encouraging, because it says that, no matter what happens to you, love is the most important thing. God created us with love and he loved us so much that he sent his Son to die for us. If it weren't for these two facts, we wouldn't have anything at all. So this is not just about romantic love, but also about the love in families and between friends—and, most importantly, the love that God has for us and that we should show to him.

When we're in love, it can be easy to spend our whole time dreaming of fairytales, reading romance novels and watching love films, but it's important for us to stay in reality, too. Romans 8:28 says, 'We know that God is always at work for the good of everyone who loves him', so ask him what good he has for you in this relationship. It might be that he wants you to learn something or wants the relationship to provide you with the support you need. It might not be right for you to know why at this moment, but ask God to teach you anything you need and keep listening to him.

Try to stay grounded by not forgetting about your other friends. When we're in love, it can be all too easy to concentrate on our boyfriend and ignore everyone else, and we don't even realise we're doing it. Make sure you spend time with your girlfriends, too, and send them texts or emails every now and then so that they know you haven't forgotten them.

When we're in love, it can also be easy to do stuff we shouldn't—particularly things of a sexual nature. God tells us that sex is only for within marriage (Genesis 2:24), as it's more than just a physical act. It's the joining of two spirits, and if we go about it in the wrong way (outside of marriage) it can really mess us up. It is difficult, but with God on our side we can do anything, including resisting temptation: as Paul writes, 'Christ gives me the strength to face anything' (Philippians 4:13).

Try not to put yourself in a situation where you could go too far. Instead of watching TV together in your room, watch it where there are other people around or go for a walk. You don't have to kill the romance—not at all! Picnics, going to the cinema, walks along the beach—they can all be romantic, and they're pretty risk-free, too. Hanging out with groups of people is good, as that way we can see our other friends at the same time, and we're not tempted to do what we shouldn't.

Dear God, thank you so much for this relationship. I pray that you will show me what you want me to learn from it and that we will go in the direction you want us to. Please help us when we feel tempted, and help us remember to keep focused on you. Amen

❊ To remember

Don't let anyone make fun of you, just because you are young. Set an example for other followers by what you say and do, as well as by your love, faith, and purity.

I TIMOTHY 4:12

❊ Reflection

- How can you live out Paul's description of love from 1 Corinthians 13 in your own life?
- What do you think God wants to give or teach you through this relationship?
- How can you make sure you keep focused on God when you're together?

When you've got an important decision to make

What the Bible says

Share your plans with the Lord, and you will succeed.

PROVERBS 16:3

Dear God, I've got a decision to make that I know is going to affect me in a big way. Please help me to make the right choices. Please help me not to worry about having to make this decision, and may I learn to trust in you more through this experience. Help me to remember, Lord, that if I stay close to you, everything will work out for the best. Amen

As we've seen, Paul, the great advice-giver of the early Church, wrote letters to the Christians in the Greek city of Corinth. In 1 Corinthians 2:10–12 he talks about God's Spirit. He says that the Spirit has shown us everything and knows everything, including what is in God's mind. Just as you are the only person who knows what goes on in your mind, the Spirit is the only one who knows what goes on in God's mind.

Paul then reminds us that God has given us his Spirit, which is why we don't think in the same way as people who don't know God—they don't have God's Spirit. He says that this is also why we recognise all the blessings that God has given us.

I like this passage because it reminds us that, as we have God's Holy Spirit, we are directly connected with God himself. The Spirit knows exactly what God is thinking and what we're thinking, all the time. So if we are in tune with the Holy Spirit, he tells us everything we need, as that is how God speaks to us and moves through us.

A lot of people find the thought of the Holy Spirit somehow

scary, but he really isn't. Old church language spoke of the 'Holy Ghost', which made people think of him as a kind of phantom that haunts us and gives us weird goosebumps. Instead, we should think of the Holy Spirit as God's breath, his way of letting us see and feel him. When you're breathing, your breath comes out, but you can only see it when it's cold and appears as condensation. I think the Holy Spirit is like that: God's always there, but we can only see him when he works as the Holy Spirit breathing on us.

When you're praying and a good idea or comforting thought pops into your head, that's the Holy Spirit. When you're worshipping and you feel really close to God, that's the Holy Spirit, too. You've probably experienced something similar even if you're not a Christian—when something suddenly clicked into place, or you felt unexpectedly calm about a stressful situation.

Anyway, because of the Holy Spirit, we can truly communicate with God, because he communicates with us in return. So when you've got an important decision to make, get God involved. Pray about the situation and ask him to send his Holy Spirit to guide you in the right direction. Make sure you listen when you pray, because that will give God space to say whatever he needs to say. It won't be an audible voice, but it could be a sense within our hearts or it could even come as words from somebody else or from a part of the Bible that you feel drawn to.

Sometimes it seems as if God isn't speaking to you, but he is always there—we can be sure of that. If we don't feel any sense of guidance, we can leave it and come back to pray more later. Often, when we're focusing hard on a question, it can be hard to hear God speaking to us, so the answer may hit us when we're not concentrating on it so much. Read some bits in the Bible (or in this book) and see whether God speaks through those words. Sleep on it, as in the morning the answer might suddenly become clear or God might give you a dream that somehow helps you to understand.

It's important to remember, when you're making big decisions, not to rush into them, as you could end up making the wrong choice out of haste. Do as much research into the different outcomes as possible, so that you're really well informed before you decide anything. Talk to friends and family about the decision, especially if they've had to make a similar decision before. Remember, though, that you have to make the choice yourself: don't do something just because other people say you should.

Don't be too concerned about making the wrong decision. Often we think we know the right way to go, but we don't do anything about it because we're afraid it will turn out wrong. Listen to your heart. If there's something that you feel strongly drawn to, and it's not just a passing whim, it's likely that it's been put in your heart by God. If you do make the wrong decision, you can always ask God for help and, if you stick by him, he'll give you plenty of chances to get back on track again.

Lord God, please be with me as I make this important decision. Help me to feel your Spirit and trust what my heart tells me to do. I thank you that you are always with me and will guide me to do what's right. Please help me to know where to turn and whom to ask for the advice I need, but also to remember that I'm the only one who can make this decision. Amen

❋ To remember

Let the Lord lead you and trust him to help.

PSALM 37:5

❋ Reflection

- What is your heart telling you that you should do? How can you make this action a real possibility?
- What is the worst thing that could happen, realistically, if you make the wrong decision? How could you make it right again?
- Are there any paths to follow that you haven't considered?

When you've achieved something good

What the Bible says

We humans are praised when we do well, and… are glad to be alive.

PSALM 49:18

Dear Lord, I thank you so much for [what I've achieved]. I feel so good about it and I want to hold on to this feeling for ever. I pray that you won't let me get big-headed because of this and that I won't get lazy now that I've achieved something. I thank you that without you I wouldn't have anything at all. Please help me to remember that. Amen

Turning again to Paul's letter to the Christians in Rome, we find him talking about gifts and achievements in chapter 12 and verses 3–11. His advice is that people should not think of themselves as being better than they really are. He speaks of the importance of using good sense and measuring ourselves in terms of how much faith we have.

He says that a body is made up of tons of different bits, each bit having its own use, and it's the same for us as human beings together. There are loads of us, but together we make up the body of Christ (the Church). Like all the bits of the body with their functions, God has given us each a gift. He says that we should use our gift for others, whether it's serving them in some way, teaching or giving encouragement.

Paul goes on to advise us that we should be honest in our love for others, hating the bad stuff and holding on to all the goodness in life. We should love each other like brothers and sisters and think more of other people than we do of ourselves. We should never give up on faith, but should follow the Holy Spirit eagerly to serve the Lord.

This Bible passage reminds us that we're all good at something, even if it's something that seems insignificant to us. It's a helpful reminder that Christians should work together, using their gifts, so that people can not only achieve things for themselves alone but the Church can achieve together, which will be even better. Science can create a bionic hand that works with motors and batteries, but it's only when it's combined with the rest of the body that it can help someone to grasp and hold and do all the things a hand is supposed to do.

I think Paul's words also remind us that when we achieve something great, or know that we have a particular gift, we should dedicate it to God in some way. So, if you've got an excellent sense of humour, use it to make people laugh and cheer them up or, if you've got a knack for giving awesome manicures, offer to paint your gran's nails for a treat. If you've achieved brilliant exam results, why not offer to help others with their homework every now and then? You might not think that you're doing anything for God, but Jesus tells us that whenever we help another person, we are helping him (Matthew 25:34–40).

When you've achieved a goal, it feels amazing and you may want to shout about it to everyone you know. While it's great to share what you've done, try not to boast too much, because that'll just make you sound big-headed. Don't forget the best person of all! God is more pleased than anyone when you succeed at something or develop a gift, so share it with him and let him into your celebration by making time to read the Bible, pray and focus your mind on him for a bit.

When you eventually come down from cloud nine, think about what you can do next. Decide what the next logical step is in terms of the gift you've got or consider something new that you'd like to try, such as learning another related (or completely different) skill. See if any of your friends would be interested in doing it with you.

Then think about how you can use your new gift in God's service.

If you're not a Christian, imagine what good stuff you can do with your new skill or development. For example, you might be able to make someone really happy or you might be able to raise money or awareness for charity. Any of these equate to the same thing.

Heavenly Father, I thank you for the gift that you have given me and all that you have allowed me to achieve through it. I pray that you will help me not to let this gift go to waste and that you will show me what I can do with it next and how I can dedicate it to you. I pray that you will help me to remember to spend time with you when I've achieved something good, Lord. Amen

❊ To remember

I would welcome an offering from anyone who wants to give something.

EXODUS 35:5

❊ Reflection

- What is the biggest gift or talent that you have been blessed with?
- How can you use it for God or to help other people?
- What new talent would you like to learn or develop? What new opportunities do you think it would bring?

When you're excited

What the Bible says

Always be joyful.

I THESSALONIANS 5:16

Lord God, I feel so excited about [what's going to happen]. Please be with me and share this happy time with me, but please also help me to be patient until that time comes and help me not to forget about you. I thank you that you are allowing me to [do this thing]. Please help me to remember that without you I would have nothing. Amen

The book of Acts tells the story of everything that Jesus' disciples did to spread the news about him after his death and resurrection. In chapter 1, verses 1–11, Luke, the disciple who wrote Acts, tells how the events started. Jesus had proved in many ways to his followers that he had risen from the dead and then told them to wait in Jerusalem for the Holy Spirit, who would show them what to do next.

Before he went to heaven, one of the disciples asked Jesus if he was now going to be their king. Jesus replied that they didn't need to know about such events, but should concentrate on the job in hand. They had to go and share the good news about him with everyone in the surrounding areas and then the whole world. After this, Jesus went to heaven in a cloud and two angels appeared to tell the disciples that that was where he'd gone.

Put yourself in their position for a moment. You finally realise that this man with whom you've spent the last three years is the Son of God, and he's proved it to you by suffering and dying in the most horrible way, then coming back to life again. Not only that, but, having come back to life, he's chosen you especially to tell everyone else about him.

You'd be pretty excited, wouldn't you? These guys didn't go around yelling their heads off as soon as they'd seen that Jesus was alive again, though. No, they did as he said and waited until the right time, until they'd been given the Holy Spirit to help them. I think this sets a good example for us, as when we're excited about something we're quite likely to get impatient and want to rush into it straightaway. We have to learn to be patient and wait for events to unfold.

It's fun to get excited about an occasion and make plans for it, but it isn't good to live in the future too much. Imagine if you were excited about going on holiday next month: it wouldn't be a good idea to pack immediately, as for the next few weeks you'd have hardly any clothes to wear. It's the same with everything: it's important (and useful) to be prepared, but if you forget about everything you have to do in the meantime, life will start to seem pretty stupid, especially once the exciting event is over.

Instead of focusing only on what we're looking forward to, we should make sure we enjoy living in the present moment, too. We need to think about all the good stuff we can do today as well. Life might seem boring until the next amazing event comes round, but we should try to appreciate all the ordinary everyday things, such as watching that TV programme we don't want to miss, eating our favourite dinner or having a laugh with our friends. That way, we won't be wishing the time would speed faster and faster away. If we constantly wish time away, before we know it, years will have gone by.

Of course, that doesn't mean we shouldn't look forward. God wants us to get excited. Matthew 5:12a says, 'Be happy and excited!'—and those are Jesus' words. Try not to forget about God and include him in your excitement. Pray to him about the situation, remembering to thank him for all the good things that are happening, and ask him to be with you throughout it. After all, it always makes us feel better if we share life with our friends, and he should be our best friend.

If you're getting really impatient, take some time out to be calm. You may just want to jump and dance around, but try to focus on something a bit quieter, too, as that will stop you feeling more and more frantic. Ask God to be with you and calm you, letting you focus on whatever is important at the present time.

Spend some time reading the Bible and look at the people in it who were really excited about stuff, such as the disciples and the writers of the Psalms, and see how they reacted. There's a lot to learn there. Let your thankfulness to God add to your excitement. Think about the fact that, if you're a Christian, starting a relationship with God will be the most exciting, life-changing thing you've ever done. If you're not feeling that enthusiasm in your faith, you may find the next chapter helpful as you try to reconnect with God.

Dear God, I thank you so much for [what I'm excited about]! I want to jump around and shout from the rooftops, but help me to be calm and to focus on everything I need to do at the moment, rather than just looking to the future. Please help me to get this excited about my faith and to feel close to you when I am bubbling over with enthusiasm. Amen

☀ To remember

Be glad that you belong to the Lord.

PHILIPPIANS 3:1A

☀ Reflection

- What good things are coming up before this exciting future event, which you can enjoy as well?
- What can you do to avoid wishing away the time before the event takes place?
- How can this exciting occasion bring you closer to God and kick-start your relationship with him?

When you're having doubts about your faith

What the Bible says

God's love and kindness will shine upon us like the sun that rises in the sky.

LUKE 1:78

Dear God, are you really there? Sometimes I feel as if you're not listening when I pray to you and that you can't help me with my problems. Please help me to feel your presence so that I can be sure you are here. Please help me through these doubts so that I can become stronger in my faith because of them. Amen

During his time of teaching, Jesus travelled all over the place with his followers. In Matthew 8:23–26, we read how Jesus and his disciples were in a boat on Lake Galilee when a really bad storm hit them and the water even started coming into the boat. While this was going on, Jesus was fast asleep.

The disciples were terrified and went to wake Jesus up, saying that they were going to drown, but Jesus replied, 'Why are you so afraid? You don't have much faith' (v. 26). Then he got up and told the storm to die down. As soon as he said this, the storm eased and everything became calm.

If you are having doubts about your faith, you might find this a really encouraging story, because it shows that even the disciples sometimes doubted Jesus' power. Also, he didn't get cross with them for doubting (or even for waking him up); he just told them that they should trust him to put it right, and he did so, straight away.

I think that God might have allowed this storm to happen in the first place so that the disciples would have an opportunity to trust Jesus. Think about it: if everything's going perfectly and you don't have anything to worry about, you don't really need to trust God very much. If you're going through an experience that's making you wonder if God's really there, it might just be that he's giving you an opportunity to put your trust in him fully. It's hard to do this sometimes, but remember that God is always there and simply continue to trust him.

Don't worry if you're having doubts. Tons of people go through exactly the same experience. Sometimes, being a Christian can feel so hard that you wonder if it's worth the struggle; sometimes you feel as if you're praying and praying but God doesn't do anything in response.

At times like this, it's important to talk to somebody you trust—a friend, a relative, someone from your church, it doesn't really matter who. Anyone who will listen to you will do. Get them to reassure you that it is normal to have these doubts (because it is!) and ask them to pray for you and help you through it.

It's also important not to give up on God. It can be hard to pray when you're struggling with doubts, but you'll end up feeling a lot better if you talk to the main person involved. Don't give up: you will get through if you persevere. If you talk to anybody who's been a Christian for any length of time, they'll tell you that they've been through phases of not being sure about aspects of their faith.

If you feel that your relationship with God is going stale, it might be worth reconsidering how you're going about it. Do you spend enough time with him? For any relationship to work, you have to spend time with the other person, so make sure you pray and read the Bible regularly. Is your church helping you? Maybe you're not feeling excited about your faith because you're in the wrong church, as far as you're concerned. Pray about it, talk with others, and consider looking at other churches to find one that will provide what you need. Just don't give up going to church altogether, because then you won't have that vital lifeline to encourage you and to get you back on track.

People have always had doubts about Jesus—even his best

friends, who followed him around for years. Just look at the disciple Thomas. Jesus appeared to the other disciples after he'd been raised from the dead but Thomas refused to take their word for it and believe, until he had touched the wounds in Jesus' side (John 20:25). Jesus didn't get cross, though; he just let Thomas do what he needed to do, so that he would believe (v. 27). People tend to be critical of 'doubting Thomas' but he can be an encouragement to us. If you're having doubts, try speaking to God about them. You can trust that he will understand and he will show you that he's there, if you'll let him. Pray that God will let you feel his Spirit so that you know his presence.

Lord God, please help me to believe and trust in you even though I can't see you. Please guide me and help me to find the right path in life and let me feel your presence so that I can be sure you are here with me, putting your loving hand on my life. Lord, please protect me and comfort me when I'm having doubts and, when I've come through my doubts, help me to learn from them and be able to help others who are in a similar situation. Thank you, Lord. Amen

☀ To remember

The Lord will hold your hand, and if you stumble, you still won't fall.

PSALM 37:24

☀ Reflection

- What is it about your faith that you're struggling with? What do you think would be the best way for you to work through this issue?
- What would you say to someone if they came and told you they were having doubts?
- What is the best thing, for you, about being a Christian?

When you want to share your beliefs with others

What the Bible says

Always be ready to give an answer when someone asks you about your hope. Give a kind and respectful answer and keep your conscience clear.

I PETER 3:15B–16

Dear Lord, please help me to be able to share my faith with the people around me. Help me not to miss opportunities to show others something of your love. I'm sorry for the times when I do miss them, and please show me some more chances so that I can keep trying. Help me to show love to everyone in all that I do. Amen

Paul wrote so much that we can read in the New Testament to encourage others and show them how to spread the word about Jesus. In 1 Corinthians 2:1–5, though, he talks about how he first started telling the Corinthian people about God, and it's really surprising! He says that when he first came to share the good news with them, he didn't use complicated words or try to sound clever, but made up his mind to speak only about Jesus, who died for us.

At first he felt weak and really scared, but when he talked he didn't try to prove anything. He simply let God's Spirit show his power through him. He says that because of this, everybody he spoke to, who came to faith, would do so because of God's power and not because of anything that humans had done.

I always find it difficult to speak about my faith to others, but this passage encourages me so much because it shows that even

Paul was sometimes scared about doing so. I think it gives us some great advice because it comes from Paul's direct experience of what worked for him. So when you want to share God's message with others, try to do what Paul says and don't overcomplicate matters. Instead, just ask God to work through you.

Sharing your faith is never easy, but it is one of our main purposes as Christians. What is the one thing that millions of people say they want more than anything? To live for ever. What can we do now that we've accepted Jesus as our Lord? Live for ever.

We should be full of joy all the time because we have the greatest gift of all—God's gift of eternal life. If only more people knew that they could be saved in this way, even from death. Well, they can—but it's up to us to tell them about it.

You don't have to stand on street corners waving a Bible and spouting scripture verses, though. That will probably just put people off. Simply allow those around you to see what you've got by being open about your faith. Be honest with your friends, family and colleagues about what you believe, if they ask you (and they will, if you pray about it). Don't be afraid to admit that you don't know all the answers. Just explain why you love God so much—and how much he loves you, as well as them.

It can be difficult to know what to say or do, and I struggle with this so much in relation to my friends and family. I'm sure I've wasted loads of good opportunities by saying stupid things. Don't worry about it, though—just keep trying, and God will provide you with opportunities when the time is right. He will also give you the words to say and the things to do, if you ask him.

Often, people think Christianity is all about staying in every night to pray and read the Bible and wearing socks with sandals and never having any fun. Of course, we know it's not like that at all! In fact, my social life has been a million times better and more fun since I became a Christian. So it's important to let people see this. Go out with your friends who aren't Christians and have a laugh with them. Maybe you could even organise a fun event through your church to show them that Christians are humans too.

Someone I'm really close to helped a friend of his to give his life to Christ without saying anything in particular. He and his best friend (who, as it happens, had brought him to faith a few years before in pretty much the same way) are just such lively people that the other friend looked at them and thought, 'Wow, I want that!'

Remember that actions speak louder than words. What we do often affects other people more than what we say, so just try to live your life the best way you can, so that your behaviour speaks about your faith for you.

It's fair to say that people generally don't want someone going up to them and telling them they're living their life wrongly and they certainly don't want to be told they're going to hell. When you want to introduce somebody to God, be very gentle. Don't let them feel that you're trying to manipulate them (because you're not—you're trying to share something fantastic with them!) and give them plenty of time to think over what you've said. If everything to do with faith is a bit of a touchy subject, do no more than drop a couple of hints every now and then. Let the other person bring up the subject first. Don't rush it; conversion can take time—sometimes years and years.

Lord God, please be with me when I am around people who do not yet know your love. Please show me how I should act so that they will warm to me and want to hear more about you. Give me patience and gentleness in how I speak to them and fill me with joy for loving you, joy that will rub off on everyone around me. I love you, Lord. Amen

❈ To remember

'Don't be afraid to keep on preaching. Don't stop!'

ACTS 18:9

※ Reflection

- What do you think are the absolute basics of the gospel message?
- Who do you know who is really good at sharing their faith? What is it that makes them so good?
- What can you do to make others see that Christianity isn't just for boring old 'religious' people?

When you want to start your journey with God

What the Bible says

Nothing is as wonderful as knowing Christ Jesus my Lord.

PHILIPPIANS 3:8A

Dear God, I'd like to know more about you and have you as part of my life. Please be with me and encourage me and show me how I can start my journey with you. Lead me in the right direction. Amen

In John 3:1–8, we read the story of one man who wanted to know more about Jesus—Nicodemus. He went to visit Jesus one night to have a chat and said that he knew Jesus had been sent by God because of the miracles he'd performed. To this Jesus replied that, in order to see God's kingdom, you have to be 'born again'.

This really confused Nicodemus and he asked how on earth he could be born for a second time. Jesus replied that, to be a part of God's people, you have to be born of the Spirit as well as in human terms. Parents can give birth to children, but only God can make someone his child. God's Spirit can give new life and, like the wind, the Spirit blows wherever it wants to.

What Jesus is saying here is that, in order to have a relationship with God, you have to start all over again. People talk about 'born again Christians', but actually all Christians have been born again. Baptism is the symbol for this new start, so Christians are baptised either as babies or when they choose faith at a later stage. I was 16 when I was baptised.

A lot of people think that Christianity is very complicated, but it's actually not at all. Here are the basics: God created the world and everything in it, but humans messed it up by choosing to go their own way. However, so that we didn't have to suffer for our mistakes for eternity, God came to earth in the human form of Jesus, where he died the most horrible death imaginable, on behalf of people like you and me, so that we could be forgiven.

That's pretty much it. The Creator of the whole universe loves you personally so much that (a) he made you and (b) he died for you. We mess up lots of times, which gets in the way of our friendships and God, but, by saying 'yes' to Jesus, all the mess gets wiped away so that we can start again. God knows absolutely everything about us, yet he still loves us and desperately wants to have a relationship with each and every one of us. (Yes, that means you!)

Having a relationship with God isn't about talking to an imaginary friend and being a complete weirdo—it's about knowing who you are, where you came from and where you're going. Pray to God; tell him that you want to start over and that you want to give your life to him. If you don't quite know what to say, use the prayer at the end of this chapter.

Start reading the Bible so that you can understand properly what faith is all about. If you don't have one, you can buy one in most bookshops or you might be able to find one at school to have a look at. Try to get hold of a youth Bible, as they're written in language that's easy to understand (rather than being full of 'thees' and 'thous'), and they often have lots of extra bits to help with life today. The Gospel of Luke is a good place to begin, as it follows the life of Jesus right through.

Talk to somebody about Christian faith. When you're starting out with anything new, it's nearly impossible if you have to do it by yourself without any help from others, so get as much encouragement as you can. Speak to anyone you know who's a Christian—a friend, a relative or even a teacher. If you really don't know where to turn, then you could try your nearest local church that holds youth events. This might sound scary but, if you speak to somebody there (especially anybody with a position of responsibility), they're sure to be more than happy to help you out.

When you want to become a Christian, church is really important, as Jesus gave us the church to be our family, to support us, comfort us and generally be there for us. A lot of people tell me that I must be really dedicated and must sacrifice a lot to go to church every week, but I don't see it like that at all because I love going. I have far more friends than I ever could have had before and, no matter what I'm going through, there is always somebody there to give me advice, to cheer me up or just to have a laugh with.

Becoming a Christian doesn't mean that you have to become a different person. God made you who you are, and he loves you for it. You can still have fun; you can still spend time with your mates; you can still go shopping and wear make-up. The only difference is that you stop living your life for yourself and start living it for God. It's not a decision to make lightly, as it is a life-changing choice, but for me it's the best thing I ever did. Why not give it a try?

Lord Jesus, I know I've messed things up in the past. I'm really sorry for it all and I want to start again, with your forgiveness. Please help me to turn away from the bad stuff that I've done and live my life for you. Thank you for dying on the cross for me. Please fill me with the Holy Spirit so that you will always be with me. Amen

☀ To remember

God loved the people of this world so much that he gave his only Son, so that everyone who has faith in him will have eternal life and never really die.

JOHN 3:16

☀ Reflection

- Which part of your past are you most ashamed of? Remember that Jesus loves you even though he knows about this, and he's ready to forgive you and help you start again.

- After reading through the bits of the Bible in this book, think about which ones appeal to you the most and why.
- Who or where can you go to, to find out more about Christianity and get the encouragement you need?

Bible index

Also from BRF

Ready to Lead

Growing Leader – Youth Edition

Ruth Hassall

There may be many reasons why you are interested in this book. Maybe someone recommended it for you, recognising that you have an ability to lead others. Maybe you are already in leadership, or you know that God has called you to be a leader and you want to grow in that role. Maybe you don't see yourself as a leader at all, but there's something inside you that wants to find out more...

This book is written for you, whichever category you are in. It explores what it means to be a young Christian leader in all kinds of settings - at church, school or college, on the sports field, even at home. It also unpacks wisdom and encouragement from 1 and 2 Timothy, two New Testament letters written by an older leader to a younger friend. *Ready to Lead* is the course book for CPAS's *Growing Leaders – Youth Edition*. It can be used a stand-alone book as well as an accompaniment to the course.

If there is an idea, invitation or opportunity that means you are becoming a leader, I highly recommend you dive into Ready to Lead *and go for it.*
IAN MACDONALD, DIOCESAN YOUTH ADVISER

ISBN 978 1 84101 620 7   £5.99
Available from your local Christian bookshop or direct from BRF: visit www.brfonline.org.uk.

Come and See

Learning from the life of Peter

Stephen Cottrell

When we look at the life of Peter—fisherman, disciple, leader of the Church—we find somebody who responded wholeheartedly to the call to 'come and see'. This book focuses on Peter, not because he is the best-known of Jesus' friends, nor the most loyal, but because he shows us what being a disciple of Jesus is actually like. Like us, he takes a step of faith and then flounders and needs the saving touch of God to continue becoming the person he was created to be.

Come and See is also designed to help you begin to develop a pattern of Bible reading, reflection and prayer. Twenty-eight readings, arranged in four sections, offer short passages from the story of Peter, plus comment and questions for personal response or group discussion.

ISBN 978 1 84101 843 0   £6.99
Available from your local Christian bookshop or direct from BRF: visit www.brfonline.org.uk.

Also from BRF

Mustard Seed Shavings

Mountain-moving for beginners

Steve Tilley

Not read any Christian book before but want to give it a go? Maybe, just maybe, this will help.

Taken a first step of faith—or a first step in taking faith more seriously—but don't quite know what to do next? Possibly you are holding something useful.

Mustard Seed Shavings offers a gentle introduction to Christian lifestyle, using the Ten Commandments as a framework. It tries to show what following Jesus means in practice today. Hopefully it reads more like receiving a present than being given a rule-book.

Each chapter ends with a pause for thought, a couple of discussion questions and a brief prayer. So, not the last word or the tiny details, but perhaps a nice place to begin.

Steve's honest and refreshing take on the Ten Commandments is guaranteed to inspire, challenge, provoke and give you a good chuckle in places. You may just find you can't put it down, but the real challenge is whether you can live it out!

MATT SUMMERFIELD, URBAN SAINTS

ISBN 978 1 84101 828 7   £6.99
Available from your local Christian bookshop or direct from BRF: visit www.brfonline.org.uk.

Enjoyed

this book?

Write a review—we'd love to hear what you think.
Email: reviews@brf.org.uk

Keep up to date—receive details of our new books as they happen.
Sign up for email news and select your interest groups at:
www.brfonline.org.uk/findoutmore/

Follow us on Twitter @brfonline

By post—to receive new title information by post (UK only), complete the form below and post to: BRF Mailing Lists, 15 The Chambers, Vineyard, Abingdon, Oxfordshire, OX14 3FE

Your Details
Name _____
Address_____
_____
Town/City _____ Post Code _____
Email_____

Your Interest Groups (*Please tick as appropriate)	
☐ Advent/Lent	☐ Messy Church
☐ Bible Reading & Study	☐ Pastoral
☐ Children's Books	☐ Prayer & Spirituality
☐ Discipleship	☐ Resources for Children's Church
☐ Leadership	☐ Resources for Schools

Support your local bookshop
Ask about their new title information schemes.